CRYPTOCURRENCY INVESTING FOR BEGINNERS

Unlock Digital Wealth with Bitcoin, Ethereum, Altcoins, and DeFi

Mark Swanson

Disclaimer:

The information provided in this book is for educational and informational purposes only and is not intended as financial advice. Please consult with a qualified financial advisor before making any investment decisions. The author, publisher, and any affiliates are not responsible for any losses or damages arising from the use of this information. Due to the rapidly changing nature of financial markets and the inherent risks in investing, readers should exercise due diligence and consult professional advisors. The author and publisher make no representations or warranties about the completeness, accuracy, or suitability of the information contained herein. Any reliance you place on such information is strictly at your own risk.

Paperback: 978-1-964863-25-2

Table of Contents

Introduction

In just over a decade, cryptocurrency has exploded from a digital curiosity into a volatile but legitimate financial phenomenon. Bitcoin, the first and most well-known cryptocurrency, was valued at fractions of a penny when it was introduced in 2009. Fast forward to today, and it has hit peaks of nearly $60,000 per unit. This meteoric rise is a clear indicator of not just the potential financial rewards of investing in digital currencies but also the broader shift towards a digital economy.

I've been engrossed in the world of cryptocurrency since its formative years. With a background in finance and a deep-seated passion for demystifying complex technologies, I've dedicated myself to helping you—whether you're a veteran investor or a curious novice—understand and navigate the ever-evolving landscape of digital currencies. My goal is not just to inform you but to empower you to make intelligent, secure investments in this dynamic market.

This book is designed to peel back the layers of what often appears to be a complex and intimidating subject—cryptocurrency investing. By breaking down complex concepts into understandable terms, I aim to provide you with the knowledge needed to participate with confidence in the digital economy. From understanding the basic technology of blockchain to learning how to safely buy and trade various cryptocurrencies, this guide covers all you need to know to start building your digital asset portfolio.

As we delve into the world of cryptocurrency together, we'll confront and debunk common myths that might have made you hesitant about digital currencies. Cryptocurrencies are not just tools for illicit trade; they are being integrated into global financial systems. By the end of this book, you'll see that digital currencies are just as much a part of our economic reality as stocks and bonds.

What sets this book apart is its focus on security and practical advice. Illustrated with real-world examples, it offers step-by-step guidance on how to make prudent investment decisions, drawing on the latest research and expert insights. This book is tailored for readers of all ages, making complex content accessible to everyone, from teens to adults.

Approach this journey with an open mind and a cautious attitude. The world of cryptocurrency is rapidly evolving, and while it offers significant opportunities, it is not without risks. Use the insights from this book to weigh your decisions and invest wisely.

Let's begin this exciting journey into the future of finance. With the proper knowledge and tools at your disposal, you are well on your way to potentially reaping the benefits of your investments in the digital age. Let this be your guide to navigating the vibrant and sometimes volatile world of cryptocurrency investing.

Chapter 1

Understanding the Basics of Cryptocurrency

Did you know that if you had invested just $100 in Bitcoin back in 2010, your investment would have soared to well over $48 million by the end of 2017? This staggering fact isn't just a testament to Bitcoin's exceptional rise; it also illustrates the immense potential of cryptocurrencies. As you step into the world of digital currencies, it's crucial to grasp the foundational concepts that underpin this innovative financial landscape. This chapter aims to demystify the basic principles of cryptocurrency, making it accessible and engaging for you, regardless of your background in finance or technology.

What is Cryptocurrency? A Simple Explanation

Definition and Origin

Cryptocurrency is defined as a virtual and/or digital currency that uses cryptography for security. Unlike traditional currencies issued by governments (fiat currencies), cryptocurrencies operate by utilizing a decentralized network of computers. This decentralization is possible thanks to a technology called blockchain, which we'll explore more in the following sections.

Cryptocurrency was first described in a 2008 paper by either an individual or group using the pseudonym Satoshi Nakamoto. The first cryptocurrency, Bitcoin, was created as a peer-to-peer electronic cash system—free from control by any institution or government. This revolutionary idea not only introduced the world to Bitcoin but also laid the foundational principles for the many other digital currencies that would follow.

Key Characteristics

Cryptocurrencies share several key characteristics:

- Decentralization: Unlike centralized banking systems, where a central authority controls and issues currency, cryptocurrencies are managed by a network system of computers known as nodes. This network works on a peer-to-peer basis, making digital currencies less vulnerable to single points of failure and censorship.

- Immutability: Once the blockchain has recorded a transaction, it cannot be altered. This immutability is ensured through cryptographic hash functions, which secure the integrity of transaction histories.

- Transparency: Each transaction on the blockchain can be seen by every participant and cannot be changed. This helps build trust among users and makes it extremely difficult to cheat the system.

Bitcoin, the first and most well-known cryptocurrency, embodies all of these principles and remains the gold standard for evaluating other digital currencies.

Use Cases

The use of cryptocurrencies has grown exponentially, extending far beyond mere investment vehicles. Here are a few practical examples:

- Online Buying: Numerous online retailers and service providers will accept cryptocurrencies such as Bitcoin, Ethereum, and others as payment, offering a secure and often cheaper alternative to credit cards or PayPal.

- Remittances: Cryptocurrencies can significantly reduce the cost and increase the speed of sending money across borders. This is particularly beneficial for migrants sending remittances back to their home countries, as it bypasses expensive and slow traditional banking services.

- Investment Vehicles: Many people buy cryptocurrencies as investments, hoping that their value will increase over time. Cryptocurrencies have also given rise to new forms of investment strategies, such as initial coin offerings (ICOs) and token sales, where investors can buy into a new cryptocurrency before it hits the market.

Advantages Over Fiat

There are several advantages to using cryptocurrencies instead of traditional fiat currencies:

- Lower Fees: Without the need for intermediaries like banks, cryptocurrency transactions can have significantly lower fees in comparison to traditional bank transfers or credit card payments.

- Accessibility: Cryptocurrencies can be particularly empowering for the population without traditional bank accounts by providing access to financial services.

- Privacy: While not wholly anonymous, cryptocurrency transactions offer greater privacy compared to traditional financial transactions, as they do not require personal information to be completed.

Blockchain Basics: How Transactions Work

Imagine a world where every financial transaction you make, from buying a coffee to selling a used textbook, is recorded in a massive ledger that is visible to everyone but owned by none. This isn't a scene from a futuristic movie; this is the reality of blockchain technology, the backbone of cryptocurrency systems. Blockchain acts as a distributed ledger, a database that is shared, replicated, and synchronized among the members of a decentralized network. The genius of blockchain is not just its ability to keep records; it's how it records and links information through cryptography, making it secure and unchangeable without the need for a central authority.

When you initiate a cryptocurrency transaction, you are essentially creating a digital 'statement,' saying, "I am sending this amount of cryptocurrency to this person." Here's where it gets interesting. Each user, or 'node.' on the cryptocurrency network has a wallet, which can be thought of as a personal ledger. Each wallet has one or more pairs of private and public keys. The public key is what you share with others to receive funds, while the private key is what you guard zealously, as it's used to approve transactions and prove ownership of the funds you are sending.

The transaction you initiate is then broadcast to the network, where it waits in a pool of unconfirmed transactions. This is where 'miners' come into play. Mining involves complex puzzles that nodes or 'miners' solve using high-powered computers. The first miner to solve the puzzle is able to add transactions to the blockchain. This process is part of what is known as the Proof of Work (PoW) consensus mechanism and is used to confirm transactions and introduce new blocks to the chain. Another mechanism, called Proof of Stake (PoS), selects validators in proportion to the number of holdings in the cryptocurrency. Both these mechanisms ensure that all transactions are verified and agreed upon by the network without the need for central oversight, thus maintaining the integrity and security of the blockchain.

Security in blockchain technology is paramount and is maintained through cryptographic hashing. Each block contains a cryptographical hash of the previous block, timestamp, and transaction data. This linkage between blocks means that to alter a single block, an attacker would need to change all subsequent blocks, which is practically impossible due to the immense amount of computational power required. This structure not only defends against fraudulent transactions but also makes the blockchain transparent and auditable by anyone in the network.

Blockchain's impact extends far beyond simply powering cryptocurrencies. Its attributes of decentralization, immutability, and transparency solve many issues of traditional transaction systems and have the potential for applications across various sectors, such as healthcare for maintaining patient records, supply chain management to track the authenticity of goods, or electoral systems to ensure secure and transparency in voting processes. This revolutionary technology fosters a level of trust and cooperation without the need for intermediaries, potentially redefining interactions in the global economy.

The Evolution of Cryptocurrencies: From Bitcoin to Today

The story of cryptocurrency begins not with a bang but with a quiet post on an obscure mailing list by someone under the name Satoshi Nakamoto. In 2008, this person or group of people issued a white paper: "Bitcoin: A Peer-to-Peer Electronic Cash System." This document laid out the mechanics of what would become the first cryptocurrency, Bitcoin. It proposed a system using a decentralized ledger—the blockchain—to record transactions securely and anonymously, bypassing traditional financial intermediaries. This was a revolutionary idea, aiming to democratize finance and reduce dependency on central banks and governments. Bitcoin officially came into existence in January 2009 with the mining of the Genesis Block.

As Bitcoin began to gain traction, it opened the floodgates for other digital currencies, collectively known as altcoins. Each of these sought to improve or diversify Bitcoin's original premise. For instance, Ethereum, introduced by Vitalik Buterin in 2015, added the capability for smart contracts, which automate transactions when certain conditions are met. Ethereum broadened the scope of blockchain applications, paving the way for decentralized finance (DeFi) and non-fungible tokens (NFTs). Ripple, another significant cryptocurrency, focused on solving problems related to international money transfers, offering a faster and more efficient alternative to systems like SWIFT. These developments marked not just technological advancements but also a growing recognition of the potential of cryptocurrencies to reshape various aspects of financial and commercial activities.

The impact of cryptocurrencies on financial markets has been profound and multifaceted. Initially viewed with skepticism, cryptocurrencies have gradually gained acceptance among both retail and institutional investors. They are now seen as a legitimate asset class, with major financial firms offering cryptocurrency-related products such as futures, options, and exchange-traded funds (ETFs). This mainstream acceptance has helped increase the liquidity and stability of cryptocurrency markets. However, it has also led to increased scrutiny from regulators and policymakers concerned about potential risks, including market volatility, investor protection, and misuse for illicit activities.

The regulatory scene for cryptocurrencies has evolved significantly over the years. Different countries have taken diverse approaches, ranging from outright bans to enthusiastic adoption. For instance, Japan recognized Bitcoin as a legal payment method in 2017, which boosted its use in the country. On the other hand, China has taken a stricter stance, cracking down on cryptocurrency trading and mining due to concerns about financial risk and energy consumption. In the United States, the regulatory environment has been somewhat ambiguous, with various federal agencies applying differing definitions and rules. The Securities and Exchange Commission (SEC), for example, has been scrutinizing ICOs and token sales to determine whether they should be classified and regulated as securities. The evolution of these regulations is a critical area of interest for investors and industry participants, as it significantly affects the development and adoption of cryptocurrency technologies.

Navigating these regulatory waters has become a key challenge for the crypto community. Each legal adjustment or new piece of legislation can send ripples across the market, influencing prices and shaping the development of new products and services. As cryptocurrencies continue to intersect more with traditional financial systems, the push and pull between innovation and regulation are likely to intensify. This dynamic creates a fascinating, albeit occasionally precarious, environment for investors and users, highlighting the need for ongoing education and cautious engagement with the crypto space.

Decoding Cryptocurrency Jargon: A Glossary for Beginners

Navigating the world of cryptocurrency can sometimes feel like learning a new language. From 'blockchain' to 'HODL,' each term carries a distinct meaning and implication that is crucial for understanding how digital currencies function and how you can interact with them effectively. Let's break down some of the key terms and phrases that are integral to mastering the language of cryptocurrencies.

Common Terms

- Blockchain: Think of it as a digital ledger or record book that is accessible to everyone but owned by no one. Every 'block' in the chain contains many transactions. Once a block is completed, it's added to the chain in a linear, chronological order. Blockchain's design makes it highly resistant to tampering, changing, or hacking.

- Mining: This is the process by which new cryptocurrency coins are made available, and transactions are verified and added to a blockchain. Miners use powerful computers to solve intricate mathematical problems that validate transactions. Successful miners are rewarded with new cryptocurrency tokens.

- Wallet: In cryptocurrency, a wallet is a digital means to store your coins securely. It's not like a physical wallet but rather a software program that holds your public and private keys, which allows you to receive and send cryptocurrencies and monitor your balance.

- Exchange: A platform allowing you to purchase, sell, or trade cryptocurrencies for additional digital currency or traditional currency, such as US dollars or Euros. These online marketplaces act like stock trading platforms.

- ICO (Initial Coin Offering): Similar to an Initial Public Offering (IPO) in the stock market. It's a way for cryptocurrency startups to raise money from the public by issuing a new token. Investors can buy these tokens, which might increase in value based on the success of the project.

Technical Concepts

- Hash Rate: This refers to the speed of a computer completing an operation in the cryptocurrency code. A higher hash rate increases the miners' opportunity to find the next block and receive a reward.

- Forks: In the cryptocurrency world, a fork happens when a blockchain's existing code is changed, resulting in two versions—one that follows the old rules and one that follows the new rules. This can be a result of disagreements within the community on certain changes in the protocol.

- Smart Contracts: These are self-executing contracts wherein an agreement's terms between the buyer and seller are written directly into the lines of code. The code and the agreements contained therein exist across a distributed, decentralized blockchain network. Smart contracts permit trusted deals to be conducted between disparate and unidentified parties without the need for a central authority, legal system, or external enforcement mechanism.

- Layer Solutions: These are technologies developed to improve the scalability and speed of blockchains. Layers built on top of existing blockchain systems provide higher transaction speeds and better scaling options.

Investment Terms

- HODL: Originally a typo for "hold" in an online forum, HODL has become a backronym for "Hold On for Dear Life." It represents a passive investment strategy where you hold onto your cryptocurrency investments despite price volatility.

- Bear/Bull Market: These terms are borrowed from the stock market. A bear market means that a market is declining, while a bull market refers to one that is rising. In the cryptocurrency context, bulls believe that the prices of specific currencies will increase, while bears believe the opposite.

- FOMO (Fear of Missing Out): The fear is that an exciting or thought-provoking event may be occurring elsewhere. This often originates in posts seen on social media. In crypto, it refers to the fear of not buying a token that might skyrocket in value.

- Whale: This term is used to describe individuals or entities that hold large amounts of cryptocurrency. These Whales have enough market power to influence the cryptocurrency market.

Security Terms

- Private Key: A sophisticated form of cryptography that permits a user to access their cryptocurrency. It's essentially your digital signature, and you should guard it with your life. If someone else obtains your private key, they can steal your crypto.

- Public Key: This acts like your bank account number. It's a way to identify your wallet so that you can receive coins. Unlike your private key, your public key is meant to be shared.

- Multi-signature Wallets: These require multiple keys to authorize a cryptocurrency transaction rather than a single signature from one key, offering added security.

- Cold Storage: This refers to keeping your cryptocurrency completely offline, which usually can be achieved through hardware wallets, USB drives, or even paper wallets. This method is particularly useful for protecting large amounts of cryptocurrency from hacking or other online threats.

Navigating through the maze of cryptocurrency terms is not just about adding new words to your vocabulary. Understanding these concepts opens up new vistas in the financial landscape, allowing you to make more informed decisions and better understand the discussions that shape the future of money. Whether you're planning to invest, use, or simply understand cryptocurrencies, getting familiar with this jargon is an invaluable part of your digital currency education.

How Cryptocurrencies Differ from Traditional Banking

The traditional banking system, as we know it, operates on a centralized model. This means that all financial transactions pass through a central authority—typically a bank or a financial institution. These entities control the flow of money, maintain transaction records, and are responsible for the security of these transactions. In contrast, cryptocurrencies introduce a decentralized model where control and verification are spread across a network of computers. This fundamental difference isn't just technical; it affects everything from how transactions are processed to how users interact with their money.

In a centralized banking system, the bank holds and controls your money. They have the authority to freeze accounts, dictate the terms of their services, and often charge fees for transactions. This centralized control also means that all your transactions are monitored by the bank and potentially by governmental bodies. Cryptocurrencies, on the other hand, offer a decentralized approach. When you use Bitcoin or any other cryptocurrency, you interact directly with the network, not a central authority. This setup empowers users with direct control over their transactions. You are able to send funds to anyone anywhere in the world without asking permission from a bank or paying exorbitant fees. This autonomy is particularly appealing in regions where the populace may not have access to traditional banking services or where the trust in financial institutions is low.

Let's talk about the efficiency of transactions. It can take days for traditional bank transfers to process, especially if they cross international borders, as they involve multiple parties and layers of bureaucracy. On top of that, each intermediary in the process adds their own transaction fees. Cryptocurrency transactions streamline this process. Because they are processed on the blockchain network, they can be completed more quickly—often within minutes—even if the transaction is international. As for the costs, because there are no middlemen setting fees, transaction fees for cryptocurrencies are typically much lower compared to traditional bank fees. This makes cryptocurrencies an attractive alternative for both everyday transactions and international remittances.

Global accessibility is another significant advantage of cryptocurrencies over traditional banking. According to the World Bank, globally, an estimated 1.7 billion adults have no access to a bank account. The reasons range from lack of sufficient funds and high fees to the geographical inaccessibility of banking services. Cryptocurrencies can change this dynamic because all you need to carry out transactions is an internet connection and a digital wallet. This accessibility has the potential to empower millions by bringing them into the global economy, fostering greater financial inclusion and independence.

Moreover, cryptocurrencies can serve regions and communities historically neglected or underserved by traditional financial systems. For instance, small business owners in remote or rural areas can accept payments in cryptocurrencies, bypassing the need for credit card processors or the high fees associated with them. Non-governmental organizations (NGOs) working in crisis-stricken regions use cryptocurrencies to transfer funds quickly and securely to areas where banking infrastructure is damaged or non-existent. This highlights not just the technical advantages of cryptocurrencies but their potential to create more equitable financial opportunities.

Cryptocurrencies are reshaping financial transactions with their decentralized nature, empowering users with more control and offering unparalleled accessibility. As we continue to explore the capabilities and potential of digital currencies, it's clear that they offer a compelling alternative to traditional banking, particularly in facilitating faster, cheaper, and more inclusive financial services. This evolution in how we think about and manage money reflects a broader shift towards a more interconnected and equitable global financial system.

Chapter 2

Setting Up for Investment Success

Imagine stepping into the world of cryptocurrency, where possibilities abound, and the promise of financial evolution is just a few clicks away. But before you dive into buying your first digital coin, you need a safe place to store it. Enter the realm of cryptocurrency wallets. Much like your physical wallet holds your cash and cards, a cryptocurrency wallet is essential for managing your digital assets. But unlike the leather-bound wallet in your pocket, digital wallets come in several forms, each with its unique features and security measures. In this chapter, we'll guide you through choosing your first cryptocurrency wallet, ensuring you start your crypto journey on the right foot.

Choosing Your First Cryptocurrency Wallet

Types of Wallets

Cryptocurrency wallets can broadly be categorized into three types: hardware, software, and paper wallets. Each type serves the same purpose but in a slightly different way, and understanding these differences is critical to choosing the right one for you.

- Hardware Wallets: Think of these as your personal crypto vaults. Small, portable devices that look much like USB drives, hardware wallets store your private keys offline, making them immune to online hacking attempts. They are considered the most secure type of wallet, especially for holding large amounts of cryptocurrency over an extended period. However, they can be a bit expensive, and their physical nature means they can be lost or damaged.

- Software Wallets: These are apps or programs that can be downloaded to your personal computer or phone. They are convenient for actively trading or spending your cryptocurrencies, as they are easily accessible. However, they are less secure than hardware wallets because they remain connected to the Internet, exposing them to potential cyber threats. Software wallets are generally free, which makes them a good option for beginners looking to start small.

- Paper Wallets: The simplest form of a cryptocurrency wallet, a paper wallet is literally just a piece of paper on which your cryptocurrency addresses and private keys are printed. They are completely offline, which makes them highly secure from online hacking. However, paper wallets are susceptible to risks like being lost, damaged, or even stolen. They are not as convenient for quick or frequent transactions and require a high level of responsibility in safeguarding them.

Security Features

When it comes to cryptocurrencies, security cannot be overstated. Here are some critical security features to look for in a wallet:

- Two-Factor Authentication (2FA): This adds an additional layer of security by necessitating not only a password and username but also something that only the user has on them, i.e., a piece of information only they should know or have immediately to hand—often a physical token.

- Multi-Signature Options: Often referred to as multisig, this feature requires multiple keys to authorize a single cryptocurrency transaction. It's like having a bank safe that needs two or three keys to open. This is particularly useful for business accounts or joint accounts, providing an extra layer of security by ensuring one person does not have complete control over the wallet's funds.

- Backup and Recovery Procedures: Always choose a wallet that offers robust backup and recovery options. Being able to recover your wallet is crucial if you forget your password or, worse, lose your device. Most wallets provide a recovery phrase—a series of words generated at random—which you must write down and store securely. This phrase is used to restore your wallet and recover your funds if needed.

Choosing the Right Wallet

Selecting the right wallet depends largely on how you plan to use your cryptocurrency. Consider the following criteria:

- Security: As discussed, the level of security is paramount. Hardware wallets offer the best security for large amounts of cryptocurrencies or long-term investments.

- User-Friendliness: Especially important for beginners, the wallet's interface should be easy to understand and navigate.

- Support for Multiple Currencies: If you plan to deal in various cryptocurrencies, look for a wallet that supports multiple currencies. This saves you the hassle of managing different wallets for different coins.

- Customer Support: Great customer support is invaluable when you're new to crypto. Check if the wallet provider offers prompt and reliable support.

Setting Up a Wallet

Setting up a cryptocurrency wallet is your first active step into the world of digital currencies. Here's how you can get started:

1. Choose Your Wallet: Based on your needs and the factors we discussed, select the type of wallet you want to use.

2. Download/Install the Wallet: For software wallets, download the app or program from a trusted source and install it on your device. Make sure you purchase your hardware wallet from a reputable vendor.

3. Set Up Security Measures: Configure all security settings available, especially 2FA and backup options. Make sure your recovery phrase is stored in a safe place.

4. Transfer Funds: Once your wallet is secure, you can transfer your cryptocurrency into it from an exchange or another wallet.

5. Keep Your Software Updated: If you're using a software wallet, regularly check and install updates to ensure your wallet's software is up to date with the latest security enhancements.

Choosing the right wallet is like finding the perfect home for your digital currencies. It's not just about keeping them safe; it's about making your experience in the crypto world as smooth and hassle-free as possible. With the right wallet in hand, you're now ready to start exploring the vast opportunities of cryptocurrency investing.

Essential Security Measures for Crypto Investors

When you step into the vibrant world of cryptocurrency, think of security as your best friend—the one who keeps you safe and guards your secrets. In this case, your 'secrets' are your investments and access keys, and your 'friend' is the robust security measure you set up to protect them. Cryptocurrency, by its very nature, offers a level of security inherently through blockchain technology. Still, fundamental safeguarding begins with how you manage your assets and interactions in the digital space.

Understanding Crypto Security

The first rule of crypto security is understanding that you are primarily responsible for it. Unlike traditional banking systems, where you can often rely on institutions to step in if things go wrong, the decentralized nature of cryptocurrencies means the onus is on you to maintain security. This begins with a clear grasp of what security in the crypto world entails—keeping your private keys private, being vigilant against scams, and regularly updating and auditing your security practices. Private keys are akin to the most personal piece of information you can hold because they provide access to your cryptocurrencies. Think of them as the combination to a safe where your digital assets are stored. Losing them to negligence or theft isn't just about losing digital data; it's about losing real money.

Protecting Private Keys

Protecting your private keys is the cornerstone of your crypto security plan. Here are some strategies to ensure they remain safe from unauthorized access:

- Use Encrypted Storage: Always store your keys in encrypted storage. This means even if someone were to gain access to your storage, deciphering your keys without the encryption key would be incredibly challenging.

- Avoid Sharing: Keep your keys confidential. The fewer people who know about where and how you store your private keys, the better.

- Physical Security: For keys stored on physical devices or paper, ensure they are kept in a secure location, such as a safe or a safety deposit box. Environmental factors like water or fire can also pose risks, so consider protective cases for added security.

- Regular Updates: Just as you might change the locks on your home if keys are lost or stolen, regularly updating your digital 'locks' or access methods can help protect against theft.

Avoiding Phishing and Scams

Phishing attacks and scams are unfortunately common in the cryptocurrency world, often designed to trick you into giving away your private keys or sending funds to fraudulent operators. Staying safe means staying informed:

- Know Common Scams: Familiarize yourself with the types of scams that are prevalent in the crypto space. These can range from fake ICOs promising incredible returns to phishing emails pretending to be from legitimate sources asking for your keys.

- Verify Sources: Always double-check the URLs of websites and the identity of people you interact with online. Scammers often create fake websites and profiles that look remarkably real.

- Think Before You Click: Be wary of links in emails or messages, especially if they ask for urgent action like providing passwords or sending funds. If you have doubts, visit the official website directly by typing the URL manually.

Regular Security Audits

Just like any good security system, your crypto defenses need regular testing and updating to ensure they can stand up against new threats. Conducting regular security audits involves:

- Reviewing Your Security Practices: Periodically review how you store and manage your keys and consider if the measures you have in place still offer adequate protection. As technology evolves, so do the tools available to enhance security.

- Updating Software: Keep all software up-to-date, including wallet software and any applications associated with cryptocurrency management. Updates may include patches for security vulnerabilities that can be exploited by hackers.

- Testing Backup Systems: Regularly test any backup systems you have in place to ensure they work effectively and that you can recover your digital assets in case of a loss or failure.

These proactive steps don't just protect your investments; they also give you peace of mind, allowing you to engage with the crypto world with confidence, knowing you've done your best to secure your digital treasure. Don't forget that in the land of cryptocurrency, your security is only as strong as the weakest link in your defense strategy. Keeping that link fortified means staying vigilant, educated, and proactive about security at all times.

Understanding Crypto Exchanges: Where and How to Buy

Navigating the landscape of cryptocurrency exchanges can feel like exploring a bustling market where each stall has its unique set of offerings and rules. Essentially, these exchanges are platforms where you can buy, sell, or trade cryptocurrencies. However, not all exchanges are created equal; they come in various forms, each catering to different needs and preferences. Let's break down the three primary types of exchanges you'll encounter and what makes each of them tick.

Centralized Exchanges (CEXs) are the most prevalent and user-friendly type of crypto exchange. They are operated by companies that provide a platform for trading cryptocurrencies in exchange for fees. These are similar to traditional stock exchanges. They act as intermediaries in your trades, providing services like order matching, currency storage, and facilitating transactions. Users appreciate centralized exchanges for their high liquidity, meaning you can buy and sell large amounts of cryptocurrency relatively easily. They also offer more advanced trading options like futures and margin trading. However, their central control becomes a double-edged sword; it introduces risks like hacking, as seen in numerous security breaches over the years. Furthermore, since they hold your funds, there's a level of trust you need to place in their security measures and business stability.

Decentralized Exchanges (DEXs) offer a stark contrast by allowing direct peer-to-peer transactions online without needing an intermediary. Here, the trades occur directly between users (peer-to-peer) through an automated process. This setup enhances security because your funds are not held by the exchange; they stay in your wallet until the transaction is executed. It also means better privacy since personal data isn't required to sign up. However, decentralized exchanges can be less user-friendly and often suffer from low liquidity and slower trade execution, which might not be ideal for those looking to make quick trades or large orders.

Hybrid Exchanges attempt to blend the best features of both centralized and decentralized exchanges. They aim to provide the liquidity and speed of a CEX with the security and anonymity of a DEX. These platforms are relatively new and are still evolving, but they represent a promising direction for secure and efficient crypto trading.

When choosing an exchange, consider several factors to ensure it meets your needs. Security is paramount; look for exchanges that employ strong security measures. For example, encryption, cold storage of funds, and two-factor authentication. Liquidity is crucial, too; a more liquid market makes it easier to trade cryptocurrencies without affecting their price too much. Fees vary significantly between exchanges and can substantially impact the cost of trading, especially if you plan to trade often or in large volumes. Lastly, user experience can dramatically influence your trading success; a well-designed interface and good customer support can enhance your trading experience.

Now, let's walk through the typical process of buying cryptocurrency on an exchange:

1. Set Up an Account: First, you need to create an account on the exchange: provide your email address, create a password, and sometimes verify your identity (known as KYC – Know Your Customer procedures), which may require a photo ID and proof of residency.

2. Fund Your Account: After your account is set up and verified, you'll need to deposit funds. Most exchanges will accept bank transfers and credit card payments, and some even support PayPal. Choose the method that aligns with your convenience and cost considerations.

3. Make a Purchase: With your account funded, you can now buy cryptocurrency. This typically involves selecting the type of currency you want to buy, specifying the amount, and executing the transaction. Some exchanges offer a simple 'buy/sell' interface, while others provide advanced trading tools and charts for more strategic trading.

4. Withdraw and Transfer: After purchasing, it's advisable to withdraw your cryptocurrency to a private wallet. Leaving your crypto in an exchange's wallet puts you at risk of losing your cryptocurrency should the exchange be hacked or go out of business. To withdraw, you'll just need to enter your private wallet's address and transfer the funds.

Navigating crypto exchanges doesn't have to be intimidating. By understanding the types of exchanges and what to look for when choosing one, you're better equipped to engage with the crypto market safely and effectively. Remember, the right exchange for you depends on your specific needs, trading style, and security preferences. Whether you opt for the convenience of a centralized exchange, the security of a decentralized exchange, or the balanced approach of a hybrid, you're now ready to take the next step in your cryptocurrency investment adventure.

Verifying Sources: Spotting Reliable Crypto Information

In the dynamic world of cryptocurrency, where fortunes can seemingly be made overnight, the information you rely on can be your greatest asset or your most significant liability. With the rapid proliferation of digital currencies and blockchain technology, there's a parallel rise in the volume of information available—some of it helpful, much of it noise, and some potentially misleading or even harmful. As an investor, whether novice or seasoned, your ability to critically assess the reliability and bias of information sources is crucial. It's akin to developing a finely tuned filter that separates the signal from the noise, ensuring you base your decisions on information that is not only accurate but also unbiased and relevant.

When evaluating sources of cryptocurrency information, consider their history, reputation, and transparency. Reliable sources typically have a track record of factual accuracy and are upfront about their ownership, funding, and editorial process. They often cite reputable sources themselves and are written by authors whose credentials and affiliations are clear and relevant to the field of cryptocurrency. Watch out for red flags such as a lack of transparency about the author or the organization, overly sensational headlines, and articles that rely heavily on anonymous sources or that fail to cite sources altogether.

Another critical skill is distinguishing between fact-based reporting and speculative hype. The crypto world is particularly rife with speculation, partly due to its relative novelty and the high volatility of digital currencies. While speculation about future prices or the potential impact of new technologies is a staple of financial reporting, it should not be confused with factual information about current events. Articles and reports should make a clear distinction between what is known and confirmed and what is conjecture or opinion. Be wary of content that presents speculative predictions with the same certainty as established facts or that bases sweeping statements on unverifiable or anonymous sources.

In terms of practical tools for verifying the credibility of cryptocurrency news, analysis, and advice, several online resources can be beneficial. Websites like CoinMarketCap provide comprehensive data on market capitalizations, pricing, and volume for various cryptocurrencies, which can help verify claims made in articles. Blockchain explorers such as Etherscan or Blockchain.com allow you to track specific transactions and view the history and distribution of blockchain assets, providing a factual basis to verify claims about transaction volumes or the movement of funds. Additionally, forums like Reddit or specialized platforms like CryptoCompare can offer community-driven insights and feedback on various sources and pieces of news.

Building a trusted resource list is an ongoing process that can significantly enhance your understanding and engagement with the cryptocurrency market. Start by identifying a few key websites, podcasts, and others with a proven track record for reliability and depth. Regularly engage with their content and monitor the accuracy of their predictions and analysis. Over time, expand your list based on references from these trusted sources or by using aggregation platforms like Feedly to discover and track new and relevant voices in the space. Remember, the goal is not to build an echo chamber but to cultivate a diverse portfolio of reliable sources that can provide you with a well-rounded view of the crypto world. This approach not only helps you stay informed but also protects you from the pitfalls of misinformation that can lead to costly investment mistakes.

Investment Mindset: Preparing for Volatility in Crypto Markets

When stepping into the ever-turbulent waters of cryptocurrency investing, understanding and preparing for market volatility is akin to wearing a life vest. The price fluctuations in crypto markets can be dizzying, with significant swings occurring within hours or even minutes. Several factors contribute to this high volatility. Firstly, the cryptocurrency market is relatively young, and with less historical data available, predictions and reactions can be extreme. Additionally, the market is heavily influenced by news and events, which can lead to rapid speculative trading. The decentralized nature of cryptocurrencies also means that regulatory news from different countries can impact prices in unpredictable ways.

For many, the rollercoaster-like nature of crypto markets can be emotionally overwhelming. It's easy to get caught up in the excitement of a surge or the panic of a drop. Here lies the importance of emotional resilience—maintaining a steady hand regardless of market conditions. Developing this strength requires a clear understanding of your investment goals and a commitment to not make impulsive decisions based on fleeting market trends. Emotional resilience in investing is about sticking to a well-considered strategy, even when your instincts might urge you to run with the crowd.

Risk management is another critical aspect of navigating crypto investments wisely. Diversification is a fundamental strategy here; don't put all your eggs in one basket. If you spread your investments across diverse assets, you can mitigate the risk of a substantial loss if one investment fails. Setting stop losses is another strategy that can help protect your investments. This involves setting a predetermined level at which your asset will be sold to prevent further loss, helping you manage and contain potential losses effectively. Moreover, it's crucial to only invest what you can afford to lose. The high volatility of the market means that investments can lead to substantial gains but also significant losses, sometimes very quickly.

Adopting a long-term perspective can also serve as a stabilizing force. While the crypto market is known for its rapid gains, it's essential to focus on steady growth over time. This perspective helps in smoothing out the highs and lows and reduces the temptation to react hastily to short-term movements. Long-term investing means being patient and waiting for your investments to mature over time, which historically has been a more successful approach than trying to time the market for quick gains.

Navigational tools and strategies such as these not only prepare you to better handle the volatility of the crypto market but also equip you to make more informed, rational investment decisions. Adopting a disciplined approach to investing, grounded in a solid understanding of market dynamics and personal risk tolerance, sets a foundation that can withstand the pressures of market fluctuations and the noise of passing trends.

In conclusion, entering the crypto market with a prepared mindset can make the difference between a precarious gamble and a calculated investment strategy.

Understanding the inherent volatility, practicing emotional resilience, applying risk management techniques, and maintaining a long-term perspective are crucial steps in cultivating a robust investment approach. As you continue to navigate through the complexities of cryptocurrency investing, these strategies will not only safeguard your investments but also enhance your overall experience in the digital finance landscape.

Moving forward, the next chapter will delve deeper into the specific tools and strategies that will help you optimize your investment decisions and manage your portfolio more effectively. By building on the foundational knowledge and mindset strategies discussed here, you'll be better equipped to engage with the dynamic world of cryptocurrencies, making investment choices that will align with your long-term financial goals.

Chapter 3

Investing Strategies for Beginners

Imagine you're in a bustling market—the colors, the noise, the myriad of options. This is somewhat like entering the cryptocurrency market, but instead of fruits and fabrics, you're dealing with a vibrant array of digital currencies, each with its potential highs and lows. Now, how do you make sense of all this? How do you pick the ripe fruits and avoid the rotten ones? This chapter is your guide to understanding and navigating the complex yet fascinating world of cryptocurrency markets. Here, we'll arm you with the basic tools and knowledge to start analyzing and making informed decisions in your investment journey.

Analyzing the Market: Basic Techniques for Beginners

Understanding the cryptocurrency market can seem daunting at first, but with the precise tools and a bit of practice, it becomes an engaging and insightful experience. Let's start with the basics—market indicators, which are essentially the vital signs of the market. These indicators include volume, price trends, and market capitalization.

Volume refers to the total number of coins that have been traded in a given timeframe. It is a powerful indicator of the activity level associated with a cryptocurrency. High trading volumes often indicate a high interest in the currency at its current price and can signify stability or potential upcoming changes in price due to increased buying or selling pressure.

Price trends provide insights into the momentum of a cryptocurrency's price. Is the price steadily increasing, or is it experiencing a downward spiral? Understanding these trends helps in predicting future movements and making decisions about when might be a good time to buy or sell.

Market capitalization, or market cap, is calculated by multiplying the current price of the currency by the total number of coins in circulation. It gives you an idea of the total value of all coins and helps gauge the scale and growth potential of the cryptocurrencies. Larger market caps usually indicate a safer investment as these markets are less susceptible to manipulation.

Now, let's talk about candlestick charts, a trader's best friend. These charts are named for their candle-like shapes, each candle providing four key pieces of information: the opening price, the closing price, the highest price, and the lowest price within a selected period. Candlestick patterns can give you insights into market sentiment and potential price movements. For example, a 'bullish engulfing' pattern suggests a potential rise, while a 'bearish engulfing' pattern might indicate a coming drop in price.

But it's not just about cold numbers and patterns; the cryptocurrency market is greatly influenced by news and global events. Regulatory changes, technological advancements, and significant shifts in investor sentiment can all dramatically affect the market. For instance, when a country announces a new regulatory framework for cryptocurrencies, it can lead to price volatility. Similarly, technological breakthroughs in blockchain, the technology underpinning cryptocurrencies, could lead to increased investor interest and a surge in price.

Sentiment Analysis

Finally, understanding market sentiment is crucial. This is the overall attitude of investors toward a particular cryptocurrency and is often influenced by news or the general economic environment. Tools, such as social media monitoring and sentiment analysis software, can help you gauge public opinion. For example, a sudden spike in positive tweets about a cryptocurrency can precede a rise in its price.

Long-term vs. Short-term Investments: Pros and Cons

Investing in cryptocurrencies can be akin to choosing between sprinting and running a marathon. Each approach, whether it's the rapid-fire trades of short-term investing or the patient journey of long-term investment, carries its own set of strategies, benefits, and challenges. Understanding these differences and determining which one aligns with your personal financial goals and lifestyle can significantly influence your success in the crypto markets.

Defining Investment Horizons

Firstly, it's crucial to understand what sets short-term and long-term investment strategies apart. Short-term investments typically refer to assets bought and sold within a short period, usually less than a year. Traders in this arena are often looking for quick profits from price fluctuations in the market. On the other hand, long-term investments are held for several years or even decades. Investors in this category are usually less concerned with short-term market volatility and more focused on the potential for substantial growth over time.

Benefits of Long-term Investing

Long-term investing in cryptocurrency can be particularly advantageous. One of the most significant benefits is the potential for higher returns. Cryptocurrencies, despite their volatility, have shown a general trend of substantial growth over the years. For instance, early investors in Bitcoin have seen their investments grow exponentially as the cryptocurrency has gained popularity and acceptance around the world. Moreover, long-term investments tend to mitigate the risks associated with the short-term volatility of the crypto market. By holding onto investments for a longer period, you're less affected by short-term fluctuations and can potentially ride out low periods until the market recovers.

Another advantage of long-term investing is the reduced impact of taxes. In many jurisdictions, long-term investments benefit from lower capital gains taxes compared to short-term investments. This can make a significant difference in your net returns. Additionally, long-term investing requires less time and energy on a day-to-day basis compared to short-term trading, which demands constant monitoring of the market and quick decision-making skills.

Risks and Rewards of Short-term Trading

While short-term trading can offer exciting opportunities for a quick profit, it also comes with its own set of challenges. The crypto market is especially unpredictable, and prices can swing wildly in short periods, making trading a high-stress endeavor. Successful short-term traders need to be skilled at reading market signals and must have the time to actively monitor trends. They also need to be disciplined enough to avoid emotional trading, which can lead to significant losses.

Moreover, short-term trading incurs higher transaction costs due to frequent buying and selling of assets. These costs can eat into your profits if not carefully managed. There's also the risk of significant losses if the market moves against you, especially if you're using leverage to increase your trading power. This can make short-term trading unsuitable for those who are risk-averse or new to cryptocurrencies.

Choosing Your Strategy

Deciding whether or not you're ready to pursue a long-term or short-term investment strategy in cryptocurrencies largely depends on your individual financial goals, risk tolerance, and time commitment. If you're looking to build wealth over time and can afford to wait out the market's ups and downs, long-term investing might be more suitable for you. This approach is generally less stressful and less time-consuming, allowing you to focus on other aspects of your life while your investments potentially grow.

Conversely, if you enjoy the thrill of trading and have the time to dedicate to studying the market and actively managing your investments, short-term trading could be rewarding. However, it's essential to have a clear strategy and to set rules for entering and exiting trades to manage risks effectively.

In either case, educating yourself about the market, staying updated with global events that could affect cryptocurrency prices, and using the right tools to analyze and manage your investments are crucial steps in achieving success. Whether you choose the sprint or the marathon, the key to profitability lies in understanding the nuances of your chosen investment horizon and aligning it with your financial vision.

Diversifying Your Crypto Portfolio to Mitigate Risks

When you first dip your toes into the vast ocean of cryptocurrency, the temptation to dive deep into popular coins like Bitcoin and Ethereum is quite strong. However, just as a diet rich in a variety of nutrients supports health, a well-diversified investment portfolio can be your best defense against the unpredictability of the market. Diversification in the context of crypto investing involves spreading your investment across different types of assets. This strategy not only minimizes your risk if one asset performs poorly but also positions you to potentially capture gains from multiple sources.

Diversification is rooted in the age-old adage, "Don't put all your eggs in one basket." In the volatile world of cryptocurrencies, this couldn't be more applicable. By diversifying, you reduce the impact that any single failing component can have on your overall portfolio. For instance, if you have invested only in Bitcoin and it experiences a sharp decline, your portfolio's value will plummet. However, if you have diversified across different asset types, a drop in Bitcoin's value might be offset by stability or gains in other crypto assets.

Let's explore the different categories of crypto assets that can add diversity to your portfolio:

• Stablecoins: These are cryptocurrencies that are pegged to a stable asset, including the US dollar, in order to maintain a consistent value. Examples include USDT (Tether), USDC (USD

Coin), and DAI. Including stablecoins in your portfolio can provide a buffer against the volatility typically associated with cryptocurrencies. They are particularly useful for managing the risks of trading and providing a safe haven during market downturns.

- Utility Tokens: Unlike coins like Bitcoin, which are primarily used as digital money, utility tokens allow users to access a product or service. These tokens are often used on decentralized applications (dApps). For example, Filecoin offers decentralized storage solutions, and its tokens are used to pay for services. Investing in utility tokens allows you to benefit from the growth of specific sectors within the blockchain ecosystem.

- Privacy Coins: These cryptocurrencies focus on providing users with greater anonymity and privacy when making transactions. Monero and Zcash are prominent examples of privacy coins. They use advanced cryptographic techniques to shield transaction details, making them attractive for users who prioritize privacy. Including privacy coins in your portfolio could hedge against potential regulations affecting more transparent cryptocurrencies.

Balancing your crypto portfolio involves more than just choosing different assets; it's about aligning your investment with your risk tolerance and goals. Start by assessing how much risk you're willing to take and what you aim to achieve with your investments. If you prefer lower risk, you might lean more towards stablecoins and established cryptocurrencies with a longer track record. Conversely, if you are inclined towards higher risk for potentially higher returns, emerging utility tokens or privacy coins might be more appealing.

Once you have selected a diverse set of assets, the next step is to decide how much to invest in each. A common strategy is to allocate larger portions to less volatile assets and smaller portions to higher-risk assets. This allocation should reflect your risk assessment and investment goals. Remember, the key is not just diversity but balance. Having a wide range of assets is futile if they don't collectively work towards achieving your financial objectives.

Rebalancing your portfolio regularly is crucial to maintaining this balance. Cryptocurrency markets can shift rapidly, and an asset that once constituted a small portion of your portfolio could grow to dominate it, skewing your intended asset allocation. When you rebalance, you ensure that your portfolio does not stray too far from your risk tolerance level. The frequency of rebalancing depends on the market's volatility and your personal investment strategy. Some investors rebalance quarterly, others bi-annually or annually. Monitoring market conditions and adjusting the frequency of your rebalancing can optimize your portfolio's performance and keep your investment strategy on track.

In essence, diversifying your crypto portfolio mitigates risk and maximizes the potential for returns. By understanding the different categories of crypto assets and strategically balancing and rebalancing your investments, you set a strong foundation for your financial growth in the crypto space. This approach not only shields you against the turbulence of a single cryptocurrency but also positions you to capitalize on opportunities across the broader crypto market.

When to Buy and When to Sell: Basic Timing Strategies

Navigating the highs and lows of the cryptocurrency market is a bit like surfing. You need to know when to paddle out and catch a wave and when it's time to ride it to shore. The trick isn't just about finding the biggest wave—it's about finding the right wave that matches your style and capabilities. In the world of crypto investments, this translates to understanding market timing, a skill that, when honed, can significantly enhance the effectiveness of your trading strategies.

Market timing is essentially the strategy of making buy or sell decisions of crypto assets by attempting to predict future market price movements. The goal is to buy at low prices and sell at high prices, but achieving this consistently over time is challenging, even for the most experienced traders. The volatility of cryptocurrency markets makes them particularly unpredictable. Therefore, it's crucial to emphasize strategy over luck, so instead of trying to perfectly time the market, which can be akin to catching lightning in a bottle, focus on developing a robust trading approach that will withstand the ups and downs, allowing you to make gains over the long term.

Implementing technical analysis tools can be immensely helpful in this regard. These tools analyze historical market data and attempt to forecast future market behavior based on patterns and indicators. For instance, moving averages is a popular tool that smooths out price data and creates a single flowing line, making it easier to identify a trend's direction. Similarly, the Relative Strength Index (RSI) can help determine whether a cryptocurrency is being overbought or oversold, suggesting potential reversal points. These tools don't provide a crystal ball into the future, but when used intelligently, they can offer valuable insights into potential market movements.

Another powerful technique in the arsenal of a crypto investor is dollar-cost averaging (DCA). This investment strategy involves regularly buying a fixed dollar amount of a particular investment, regardless of the share price, thereby reducing the impact of volatility on the overall purchase. The purchases occur at regular intervals and in equal amounts. If the market is down, your fixed dollar amount will buy more shares, and vice versa when the market is up. DCA can help lower the average cost per share of the investment over time, potentially reducing the risks and smoothing out the investment's performance. This is a particularly useful approach in the cryptocurrency market, known for its sharp highs and lows, as it mitigates the risk and takes the emotion out of investing.

Setting up buy or sell triggers can also streamline your trading decisions. These are automated rules that you set up on your trading platform to execute buy or sell orders when certain conditions are met. For example, you might set a buy trigger when a particular cryptocurrency drops to a specific price or a sell trigger when it rises to a certain price level. These triggers are based on your analysis and understanding of the market, and once set, they can help automate your trading strategy, allowing you to capitalize on market movements even when you're not actively monitoring the charts. This method not only saves time but also ensures that your emotions don't cloud your trading decisions.

Incorporating these strategies into your trading approach can help you make more informed and timely decisions and will enhance your ability to capitalize on market opportunities. While perfect timing is unattainable, equipping yourself with the right tools and strategies can increase your chances of success, making your trading journey not only more strategic but also more rewarding. Remember, in the fluctuating seas of cryptocurrency trading, using the correct navigational tools can make all the difference.

Using Tech Tools: Apps and Platforms for Market Analysis

In the vibrant and ever-evolving world of cryptocurrency, staying current with the newest market trends is critical. Thanks to technological advancements, a plethora of tools have been developed to aid investors in navigating these waters. These tools range from comprehensive desktop platforms to handy mobile apps, each equipped with a suite of features designed to streamline the analysis process. Understanding what each tool offers and how to effectively use them can significantly enhance your trading strategies and market understanding.

When exploring the landscape of market analysis tools, you'll encounter a variety of applications designed to cater to different aspects of trading and investment analysis. Popular platforms like TradingView and Coinigy are favorites among many traders for their in-depth charting capabilities and real-time data analytics. These platforms offer a broad range of features, including price charts for various cryptocurrencies, drawing tools, and even community forums where traders can exchange insights. Another helpful tool is CryptoCompare, which provides a comprehensive overview of cryptocurrency markets with data on price movements, volumes, and market cap across multiple exchanges.

Key features to look for in these tools include user-friendly interfaces that make navigation and comprehension easy, even for beginners. Alert systems are another essential feature; they notify you about significant price changes or when specific market conditions are met, helping you to act swiftly on potential trading opportunities. Integration with trading platforms is also a critical feature, allowing you to make trades directly from the analysis app. This integration streamlines the process, minimizing the time lag between decision-making and action, a crucial aspect in a market as volatile as cryptocurrency.

The choice between mobile and desktop applications depends mainly on your lifestyle and trading style. Mobile apps offer the advantage of accessibility and convenience. With a mobile app, you can monitor markets, execute trades, and receive alerts on the go, ensuring you never miss a beat, no matter where you are. Apps like Blockfolio and Delta are particularly popular among mobile users for their sleek interfaces and comprehensive tracking features that allow you to manage your portfolio from your smartphone.

However, desktop platforms often provide more robust analytics tools and a more stable environment for detailed analysis. They are particularly beneficial for those who engage in complex trading strategies that require multiple screens or detailed chart analyses. Desktop applications typically offer more charting options and a broader array of analytical tools compared to mobile apps, making them suitable for in-depth technical analysis.

Safety and security should never be compromised when choosing a tech tool for market analysis. The cryptocurrency market's decentralized nature makes it a prime target for cyber threats. Opt for platforms that prioritize security, offering features like two-factor authentication (2FA), encryption, and secure data storage. It's also prudent to conduct due diligence on the tool's developer, ensuring they have a solid reputation and a transparent privacy policy. Regularly updating the software is crucial to protect against vulnerabilities and ensure you are using the most secure and efficient version of the tool.

Incorporating these technological tools into your market analysis strategy can transform the way you interact with the cryptocurrency market. They not only provide you with real-time data and in-depth analysis but also enhance your decision-making process, allowing you to respond more effectively to market changes. As you become more familiar with these tools, you'll find yourself better equipped to manage your investments and capitalize on opportunities that you might have otherwise missed.

Navigating through the dynamic world of cryptocurrency can be daunting, but with the right tools at your disposal, it becomes a manageable and even enjoyable endeavor.

The tools and platforms discussed in this chapter are designed to enhance your understanding of the market, streamline your trading processes, and secure your transactions. From mobile apps that offer convenience and quick access to desktop platforms that provide comprehensive analysis and robust features, these technological solutions are invaluable for anyone looking to succeed in the crypto market.

As we wrap up this chapter, remember that the goal is to use these tools to inform and enhance your investment strategies, not to replace your judgment. Each tool offers different capabilities and may suit different trading styles and needs. Experiment with a variety of tools to find what works best for you, and always stay informed about new technological advancements that could further optimize your trading experience.

Looking ahead, the next chapter will delve into the psychological aspects of trading, exploring how emotions can influence decision-making and how to cultivate a mindset that fosters successful investment strategies. This exploration is crucial, as the mental and emotional demands of trading can be just as challenging as the technical aspects covered so far.

Chapter 4

Dealing with Risks and Scams

Navigating the exhilarating world of cryptocurrency is a lot like exploring uncharted waters—thrilling and potentially rewarding, but not without inherent risks. As you chart your course through these digital seas, it's crucial to be aware of the pirates lurking in the shadows: scams and fraudulent schemes that aim to part you from your hard-earned treasure. In this chapter, we'll delve deep into the common pitfalls that every cryptocurrency investor should be wary of and equip you with the tools and knowledge to steer clear of them. By understanding these risks, you'll be better prepared to safeguard your investments and navigate your way to safer harbors.

Identifying and Avoiding Common Cryptocurrency Scams

Types of Scams

The world of cryptocurrency, while full of opportunities, is also a fertile ground for various types of scams. These fraudulent activities can vary widely in their approach and sophistication, but some of the most common include:

- Phishing Scams: These occur when scammers create fake websites or send emails that mimic legitimate businesses to steal personal information or login credentials. They often urge you to act quickly, offering a false sense of urgency to trick you into providing sensitive information.

- Fake ICOs: Initial Coin Offerings (ICOs) can be an authentic way for new projects to raise funds. However, counterfeit ICOs are set up by scammers who use the hype around new launches to lure investors into buying nonexistent tokens. These can often be spotted by their lack of detailed documentation or unrealistic promises about returns.

- Ponzi Schemes: In a Ponzi scheme, returns are paid to earlier investors using the capital of newer investors. These schemes lead you to believe that profits are coming from product sales or other means, while in reality, they're dependent on an ever-increasing flow of new investors.

- Fraudulent Exchanges: Some platforms may pose as legitimate exchanges to lure users into depositing funds, which are then stolen. These fake exchanges might offer features that sound too good to be true or may have very little to no user feedback.

Red Flags

Recognizing the red flags can help you avoid falling victim to these scams. Be cautious of:

Guaranteed Returns: In the world of investing, there are no guaranteed returns. Any promise of guaranteed profits should be treated as a major red flag.

Unsolicited Offers and High-Pressure Tactics: Be wary of unexpected offers, especially those that pressure you to make a quick decision.

Scammers often create a sense of urgency to push you into making decisions without due diligence.

Lack of Transparency: Genuine projects are transparent about their processes and who their team members are. A lack of clear information about the project's team, location, or how it works should raise suspicions.

Preventive Measures

To safeguard yourself against these dangers, consider the following preventive measures:

- Verify Legitimacy: Always check the credibility of the platforms or ICOs. Look for reviews, user feedback, and news articles. Visit forums like Reddit or BitcoinTalk, where the community discusses new projects.

- Use Two-Factor Authentication (2FA): Adding an extra layer of security can protect your accounts even if your password is compromised.

- Conduct Thorough Research: Before investing, research thoroughly. Check multiple sources and make sure you understand how the investment works. If the project is genuine, there will be plenty of verifiable information available.

Resources for Verification

To help you verify the credibility of crypto projects and offers, utilize resources such as:

- Blockchain Explorers: Tools like Etherscan or Blockchain.com allow you to track transaction histories and wallet balances, helping you verify the claims made by investment projects.

- Reputable Crypto News Websites: Websites like CoinDesk, CoinTelegraph, and CryptoSlate offer up-to-date news on the cryptocurrency world and can be a reliable source of information on new projects and potential scams.

- Regulatory Announcements: Keep an eye on announcements from financial regulators about new rules or warnings regarding cryptocurrencies and ICOs.

Visual Element: Checklist for Avoiding Crypto Scams

To simplify the process of identifying and avoiding scams, here's a handy checklist that you can refer to whenever you encounter a new investment opportunity:

1. Verify the URL: Ensure the website link is correct and not a close imitation of a well-known site.

2. Look for Secure Connections: Check for 'https' in the web address—a sign of a secure connection.

3. Research the Team: Look for clear information about the project team and their credentials.

4. Read the Whitepaper: Every legitimate project should have a detailed whitepaper. Read it thoroughly.

5. Check Token Economics: Understand how the tokens are distributed and what controls inflation.

6. Seek Community Feedback: Explore forums and social media to see what others are saying about the project.

This checklist can serve as a quick reference to ensure you're conducting the necessary due diligence before committing your funds to any crypto project. Remember, in the world of cryptocurrency, being well-informed is your best defense against scams. By taking proactive steps to verify the information and understand the investments you are considering, you can navigate this dynamic space with confidence and security.

The Importance of Regulatory Compliance in Crypto

Attempting to understand the global regulatory landscape for cryptocurrencies is akin to navigating a complex maze—each turn representing different national laws and international guidelines that directly impact how you engage in crypto trading and investment. Across the globe, the regulatory approach to cryptocurrencies varies widely; some countries embrace them, others regulate them heavily, and a few even ban them outright. For instance, in the United States, cryptocurrencies are treated both as commodities by the Commodity Futures Trading Commission (CFTC) and as property for tax purposes by the IRS. On the other hand, countries like Japan have acknowledged Bitcoin and other digital currencies as legal property and have a relatively straightforward regulatory framework that governs their trade. Conversely, China has taken a much stricter stance by banning all cryptocurrency exchanges and Initial Coin Offerings (ICOs) within its borders.

The impact of these regulations on investors cannot be overstated. Compliance with local and international regulations not only helps in avoiding legal pitfalls but can also significantly protect investors from fraud. Regulations require exchanges and ICOs to implement stringent security measures, conduct thorough audits, and maintain transparent operations. These regulations work to stabilize the crypto market by reducing fraud and increasing investor confidence. For instance, when exchanges comply with Anti-Money Laundering (AML) and Know Your Customer (KYC) regulations, it ensures that the platforms are not being used for illegal activities like money laundering. This compliance protects investors by ensuring that the platforms are safe and reputable, thereby safeguarding investor funds.

Navigating this complex regulatory environment requires a proactive approach. Start by educating yourself on the regulations that apply in your country and any other regions where you intend to trade. This knowledge is crucial as it directly affects how you report taxes, the legality of your transactions, and the types of crypto-related activities you can legally participate in. For US residents, this means understanding the reporting requirements set by the IRS regarding gains made from cryptocurrency transactions. In the European Union, you'll need to be aware of the Fifth Anti-Money Laundering Directive (5AMLD), which includes stricter transparency requirements.

Staying updated with regulatory changes is equally crucial. The world of cryptocurrency is fast-paced, with new technological advancements and regulatory changes occurring regularly. Subscribe to newsletters from regulatory bodies such as the Securities and Exchange Commission (SEC) in the US or the Financial Conduct Authority (FCA) in the UK. Following trusted crypto regulatory analysts on social media or professional networking sites like

LinkedIn can also provide timely updates and expert insights into how new regulations could affect your investment strategy.

Moreover, for international traders, understanding the global regulatory landscape is essential. The G20 countries, for example, have been working towards creating a unified framework that addresses the issues of crypto-assets. Being aware of such developments can help you anticipate changes in your home country's regulations and prepare accordingly.

Navigating compliance might seem daunting, but it is a fundamental aspect of engaging with cryptocurrencies safely and successfully. By understanding and adhering to the regulations, you not only protect yourself from legal repercussions but also contribute to the legitimacy and stability of the broader crypto market. Your proactive efforts in staying informed and compliant not only safeguard your investments but also enhance your credibility and reputation in the crypto community. As the regulatory landscape continues to evolve, your ongoing commitment to compliance will remain a cornerstone of your successful engagement with the world of cryptocurrency.

What to Do If You Suspect a Crypto Scam

Imagine you're browsing through your emails or scrolling through a social media feed, and you stumble upon an offer or an investment opportunity that seems a bit off. Maybe the promises seem too good to be true, or perhaps there's an unexpected urgency to act. You may have just encountered a crypto scam. Knowing what to do next can not only potentially save you from financial loss but also contribute to a safer crypto community by helping to expose fraudulent schemes.

The first step if you suspect a scam is to disconnect immediately. If you're on a website, close it; if you're in an app, exit. Do not click on any more links, and definitely do not provide any personal information or make any payments. If you've already shared some data or made a transaction, it's crucial to secure your assets next. Move your funds to a new wallet with a strong and unique password. If you suspect your financial information has been compromised, alert your bank or credit card company immediately to place holds on your accounts.

After you've secured your assets, it's time to report the scam. This is vital because timely reporting can help authorities catch the perpetrators and prevent them from harming others. Start by documenting everything about the scam, including emails, website links, social media posts, and any communications. Screenshots and URLs are particularly useful. Then, report the scam to the relevant authorities. In the United States, this could be the Federal Trade Commission (FTC) through their website or the Internet Crime Complaint Center (IC3). Many other countries have similar governmental bodies that handle fraud reports. Additionally, if the scam occurred on a social media platform or involved a specific cryptocurrency exchange, report the incident to those entities as well. Most platforms take these reports seriously and can take action to prevent further scams.

Seeking professional help is also a wise step, especially if significant assets are involved or if the scam has legal implications. A legal professional, particularly one with experience in fraud or cybercrime, can provide advice tailored to your specific situation. They can help you understand your rights and the possible recourse available to you. In some cases, they might even be able to help you recover lost funds. Additionally, consulting with a cybersecurity expert can help you secure your digital presence to prevent future incidents.

Finally, consider sharing your experience with the community. While it might feel uncomfortable to admit that you were targeted, publicly sharing your story can be incredibly beneficial to others. It raises awareness about the tactics scammers use and educates the public on how to recognize similar scams. You might opt to write a blog post, share an update on social media, or even speak at community events. Remember, every piece of shared knowledge contributes to a more informed and prepared community, making it harder for scammers to find victims.

Navigating through a suspected scam can be stressful and intimidating, but taking these steps will not only help to protect your assets but also contribute to the broader fight against cybercrime in the cryptocurrency space. By acting swiftly to disconnect and secure your assets, diligently reporting to authorities and platforms, seeking the right professional advice, and courageously sharing your experience, you play a crucial role in fortifying the defenses of the entire crypto community against fraudulent activities.

Risk Management Strategies for Crypto Investors

Navigating the cryptocurrency market effectively demands more than just knowing the best times to buy or sell. Having robust risk management strategies is like setting up guardrails on your investment journey—they don't obstruct the view but ensure you don't veer off the path during unexpected conditions. Let's explore some fundamental concepts and practical strategies in risk management that can safeguard your investments in the volatile world of cryptocurrency.

Fundamentals of Risk Management

Risk management in cryptocurrency investing involves identifying, assessing, and controlling threats to your capital. These risks can stem from market volatility, regulatory changes, technological failures, and security breaches, among other factors. Effective risk management starts with acknowledging that investments can go down as well as up, and some level of risk is always involved. Therefore, the goal is not to eliminate risk but to manage it intelligently to balance potential rewards with your tolerance for potential losses.

One fundamental concept here is the 'risk-reward ratio,' which investors use to compare the expected return of an investment with the amount of risk undertaken to capture this return. For instance, if you're eyeing a cryptocurrency with potentially high returns, it's crucial to assess whether the high volatility and possible losses are acceptable to you. Setting clear goals and knowing your financial threshold can help guide this decision-making process.

Diversification Strategies

Diversification is one of the most effective strategies used to manage investment risks. It involves spreading your investments across various asset types to reduce exposure to any single asset or risk. In the context of cryptocurrency, this could mean investing in different types of digital assets like Bitcoin, and Ethereum, altcoins with different functionalities, and even tokens from emerging sectors like DeFi (Decentralized Finance) or NFTs (Non-Fungible Tokens).

However, proper diversification also extends beyond crypto assets. Incorporating non-crypto investments like stocks, bonds, real estate, or commodities can provide a buffer against crypto market volatility. This blend of asset types tends to react differently to the same economic event, which can help stabilize your overall portfolio performance during market swings.

Utilizing Insurance Options

As the crypto ecosystem matures, more sophisticated risk management tools are becoming available, including insurance. Crypto insurance can protect against a variety of risks, including theft, hacking, and even the loss of access to your crypto due to forgotten passwords or failed hardware. Several companies now offer policies designed specifically for digital assets.

Choosing the right insurance policy involves understanding what's covered and what's not. Most policies cover the theft of digital assets up to a certain limit and under specific conditions. It's essential to work with insurers who understand the nuances of cryptocurrency and can provide policies that match your investment profile. Always read the terms carefully and consider whether the premium costs are justified by the coverage provided.

Building a Risk-Aware Culture

Maintaining a risk-aware culture is essential, especially in a field as young and rapidly evolving as cryptocurrency. This involves staying educated about market developments, understanding the technologies behind your investments, and staying alert to changes in the regulatory landscape that could affect your holdings.

Continuous education is critical, whether it's through reading up on new technologies, participating in community discussions, or following thought leaders and experts in the field. The more informed you are, the better equipped you'll be to make decisions that align with both market conditions and your personal investment goals.

By integrating these risk management strategies—understanding fundamental principles, diversifying your portfolio, utilizing insurance options, and fostering a risk-aware culture—you can navigate the crypto markets more safely and confidently. These strategies not only protect your investments but also give you a firmer foundation for exploring new opportunities in the dynamic world of cryptocurrency.

As we close this chapter, remember that managing risk is not about avoiding it but understanding and controlling it to your advantage. The strategies discussed here are tools to help you build resilience against the uncertainties of the market. In the next chapter, we'll shift our focus to advanced investment strategies that can further enhance your ability to capitalize on market opportunities while managing risk effectively.

Chapter 5

Beyond Basic Investments

The world of cryptocurrency offers a landscape ripe with opportunities for those willing to explore beyond the traditional pathways of buying and trading digital currencies. One of the most captivating developments in this dynamic field is the emergence of Non-Fungible Tokens or NFTs. Imagine owning a digital piece of art that, unlike any print or replica, is uniquely yours or holding a virtual real estate property in a digital world. This isn't a futuristic fantasy; it's a reality made possible by NFTs, transforming how we perceive ownership and value in the digital age.

Introduction to NFTs: Buying, Selling, and Trading

Understanding NFTs

Non-Fungible Tokens (NFTs) are digital assets that denote ownership of unique items or content, using blockchain technology to certify authenticity and ownership. Unlike cryptocurrencies like Ethereum or Bitcoin, which are fungible, this means that each unit is the same as every other unit; each NFT is unique, has distinct properties, and isn't interchangeable. This uniqueness is what gives NFTs their value, particularly in realms like digital art, collectibles, and virtual real estate. For instance, an NFT could represent an original digital painting, a one-of-a-kind virtual trading card, or an exclusive piece of virtual land in a blockchain-based online world.

How to Buy and Sell NFTs

The process of buying and selling NFTs typically takes place on specialized platforms that act somewhat like digital art galleries or collectible marketplaces. Some of the most popular platforms include Foundation, OpenSea, and Rarible. Here's how you can start your journey into the world of NFTs:

1. Set Up a Digital Wallet: You will need a digital wallet before you can trade NFTs: one that supports Ethereum, as most NFT platforms are built on the Ethereum blockchain. This wallet will be used to store your NFTs and process transactions.

2. Choose a Platform: Select an NFT marketplace that aligns with the type of digital asset you're interested in. Each platform has its own set of rules and fees and caters to different types of NFTs.

3. Create or Buy NFTs: If you're an artist or creator, you can perfect your own NFTs on these platforms, turning your digital art or collectibles into purchasable assets. If you're looking to buy, you can browse the marketplace for NFTs that catch your eye and purchase them using cryptocurrency.

4. Consider Transaction Fees: Be aware of the fees involved. Most NFT transactions require a 'gas' fee, which is a payment made to compensate for the computing energy required to process and validate transactions on the blockchain.

Market Trends and Valuation

The valuation of NFTs can be influenced by various factors, from the fame of the creator and the uniqueness of the content to the potential for future appreciation and the overall demand within the NFT market. For instance, an NFT created by a well-known digital artist may command a higher price than one by an emerging artist. Similarly, an NFT representing a key plot in a popular virtual world might be more valuable than a more common offering.

It's crucial to closely watch market trends. Platforms like NonFungible.com provide valuable data on market trends, sales, and average prices, helping you make informed decisions. Whether you're buying for personal enjoyment or investment potential, understanding these dynamics can enhance your ability to choose wisely and invest effectively.

Risks and Legal Considerations

While the NFT market offers exciting opportunities, it also comes with its share of risks and legal complexities. Market volatility is a significant factor; the value of NFTs can fluctuate wildly based on market trends and consumer interest. Additionally, copyright and ownership issues can pose legal challenges. It's crucial to verify the authenticity and copyright status of an NFT before purchasing. Ensure that the token you're buying genuinely represents the ownership rights it claims, and be aware of the legal implications, especially if you plan to reproduce or monetize the NFT.

Understanding these aspects of NFTs—from the basic functioning and trading process to the nuanced dynamics of market valuation and legal considerations—can equip you with the knowledge to navigate this innovative field. As you delve into the world of NFTs, remember to approach with curiosity and caution, balancing the allure of unique digital assets with a sound understanding of their value and risks.

Visual Element: Infographic on Steps to Buy and Sell NFTs

To help you visualize the process, here's an infographic that breaks down the steps to buying and selling NFTs. This visual guide provides a quick reference to ensure you have the essential information at your fingertips, simplifying your entry into the NFT market. Whether you're an artist looking to mint your first digital creation or a collector eager to explore unique digital assets, this guide aids in navigating the exciting realm of NFTs with confidence and ease.

Decentralized Finance (DeFi): An Emerging Frontier

Imagine a financial system where every transaction, agreement, and operation is transparent, easily accessible by anyone in the world, and operates without the need for traditional banks or financial intermediaries. That's the revolutionary promise of Decentralized Finance, commonly referred to as DeFi. Built on blockchain technology, particularly Ethereum, DeFi offers a global, open alternative to every financial service you use today—from savings, loans, and trading to insurance—and allows them to operate independently and more efficiently. This system isn't just for the tech-savvy or the financially privileged; it's designed to be accessible to anyone with an internet connection, fundamentally changing how we think about and interact with money.

DeFi uses smart contracts, which are self-executing contracts with the terms of the agreement directly written into the lines of code. These contracts operate on public blockchains, making them accessible to everyone but also irreversible and secure. These features form the backbone of various DeFi applications that aim to replicate and improve upon the services offered by traditional financial institutions.

Core DeFi Applications

One of the most common applications of DeFi is lending platforms. Platforms like Aave or Compound allow users to lend out their cryptocurrencies, like lending out money in a savings account, to earn interest directly from the borrower. What makes DeFi lending different is that it's entirely over-collateralized, meaning the borrower must lock up a higher amount of cryptocurrency than the amount they are borrowing. This collateral can be liquidated by the platform to pay back the lenders if the borrowers fail to uphold their side of the deal.

Another cornerstone of DeFi is decentralized exchanges (DEXs). Unlike traditional exchanges, DEXs allow users to trade cryptocurrencies directly without needing an intermediary to hold their funds. Platforms like Uniswap or SushiSwap use smart contracts to create liquidity pools that automatically execute trades based on pre-set algorithms. This not only speeds up the trading process but also increases security, as the tokens remain within the users' control, held by smart contracts rather than by the exchange.

Yield farming, a newer application, involves users moving their cryptocurrencies around between different lending and trading platforms to maximize their returns from DeFi lending and trading opportunities. It's akin to moving money between various bank accounts to take advantage of the best interest rates available, but it's executed in a way that's automated and can interact with multiple platforms at once.

Participating in DeFi

Getting involved in DeFi starts with setting up a digital wallet that will support Ethereum, such as MetaMask, Trust Wallet, or Coinbase

Wallet. These wallets not only store your cryptocurrency but also interact with DeFi applications directly through their interfaces. Once you've set up your wallet, you can connect it to a DeFi platform by visiting the platform's website and linking your wallet.

When you start interacting with DeFi platforms, you'll encounter transaction fees known as gas fees, which are payments made in compensation for the computing energy used to process and authenticate transactions on the Ethereum network. These fees will vary based on network demand and can become relatively high during peak times, so it's crucial to consider these costs when you're making transactions.

Security Practices in DeFi

While DeFi opens up enormous opportunities, it also comes with its set of risks, primarily technical risks from smart contract vulnerabilities. Smart contracts are only as secure as the code they are written with, and if there are bugs in the code, it can lead to funds being lost or stolen. Therefore, it's important to engage only with platforms that have undergone rigorous security audits by reputable firms.

It's also wise to diversify your DeFi interactions and not lock all your funds in a single platform or contract. Just as you wouldn't invest all your money in a single stock, you shouldn't expose all your digital assets to the risks of one single DeFi project.

The world of DeFi is still in its infancy but is rapidly evolving, continuously enhancing its protocols to offer more secure and effective financial services. By ensuring you understand the platforms and the technologies behind them, you can take advantage of what DeFi has to offer while mitigating the risks involved. Whether you're looking to earn interest on your crypto assets, borrow funds, trade tokens, or explore new financial products, DeFi provides a powerful, accessible set of tools that reimagines the future of finance.

Staking Cryptocurrencies: Passive Income Explained

In the evolving landscape of cryptocurrency investment opportunities, staking emerges as a compelling method to not only support the operational and security mechanisms of blockchain networks but also to earn rewards. Simply put, staking involves holding funds in a cryptocurrency wallet to support the operations of a blockchain network, and, in return, you receive a reward, much like interest in a traditional bank savings account. This process is particularly associated with cryptocurrencies that use the Proof of Stake (PoS) model. Unlike the energy-intensive Proof of Work (PoW) model used by Bitcoin, which requires computational power to mine new coins, PoS relies on participants holding stakes in the coin to validate transactions and create new blocks.

The allure of staking lies in its dual benefit: contributing to the blockchain's efficacy and security and earning potential passive income through staking rewards. However, the process and profitability of staking can vary significantly based on the cryptocurrency and the staking method chosen. Let's delve deeper into how you can engage with staking, the different approaches available, and the considerations you should keep in mind to optimize your staking strategy.

Choosing a Staking Option

Staking can be approached in several ways, each with its nuances. Direct staking involves participating directly in the blockchain by holding and offering your coins directly from your wallet. This method often requires meeting a minimum number of coins and running a node, which can be technical and may not be suitable for everyone.

Staking pools, on the other hand, are a more accessible option. They involve pooling your coins with other investors to increase your chances of validating blocks and earning rewards. Staking pools are managed by third parties and reduce the technical barriers associated with setting up nodes, making them a popular choice for individuals who may not have enough coins to meet the minimum requirements for direct staking or the technical expertise to run a node.

Third-party staking services offered by some cryptocurrency exchanges allow you to stake your coins directly through the platform. While this method offers convenience, it often comes with fees and somewhat less control over your staked assets. It's crucial to choose reputable services if you opt for this method, as the security of your staked assets depends on the platform's robustness.

There are pros and cons to each staking method. Direct staking gives you complete control and potentially higher rewards, but it's technically challenging and has higher entry requirements. Staking pools offer simplicity and lower entry barriers but may come with pool fees and slightly lower rewards due to distribution among more participants. Third-party services provide convenience but at the cost of control and potential platform risks.

Risks Involved in Staking

While staking offers numerous benefits, it's not without risks. Liquidity issues can arise, as staked coins are locked up and cannot be sold or moved until the end of the staking period, which might prevent you from accessing your assets quickly in volatile markets. Slashing is another risk, particularly in direct staking scenarios, where validators can lose a portion of their staked coins if they fail to validate blocks correctly or attempt to corrupt the network.

Additionally, the responsibility of running a node, if you are staking directly, includes ensuring your node is always online and functioning correctly, as downtime can also lead to penalties or reduced rewards. These risks necessitate a careful approach to staking. Ensuring regular updates and maintenance of your hardware and software, choosing reputable staking pools or platforms, and staying informed about the staking protocol and network conditions can help mitigate these risks.

Expected Returns

The potential returns from staking can be attractive, but they vary widely depending on the coin, the amount staked, network conditions, and the inflation rate of the staked asset. Generally, staking rewards can range from a modest 5% to an impressive 20% annual return, sometimes even higher. However, these returns are not guaranteed and can fluctuate based on the factors mentioned above. To set realistic expectations, it's advisable to research historical returns, understand the specific staking requirements and reward mechanisms of the blockchain you're interested in, and also consider the potential impact of market volatility on the value of your staked coins.

Staking stands out as a relatively accessible means of earning passive income while participating in the cryptocurrency ecosystem. It allows you to support the security and operability of blockchain networks while potentially growing your digital assets. Whether you choose direct staking, join a staking pool, or use a third-party service, understanding the intricacies of each method and the associated risks is crucial. With careful consideration and strategic planning, this can be a valuable addition to your cryptocurrency investment portfolio, aligning the growth of your assets with the advancement of blockchain technology.

Crypto Crowdfunding: Participating in ICOs Safely

In the bustling universe of cryptocurrency, Initial Coin Offerings (ICOs) represent a fascinating frontier of opportunity for both creators and investors. Much like a traditional IPO gives investors a chance to buy shares in a company, an ICO is a mechanism through which new crypto projects raise capital by issuing their own digital tokens to early backers. This form of crowdfunding is fueled by blockchain technology, which ensures the transparency and safety of transactions. Unlike traditional fundraising methods, where investors receive shares of a company, ICO participants are usually motivated by the potential utility of the token in the ecosystem being developed or by the prospect of the token gaining value over time.

Understanding the mechanics of ICOs is crucial before you decide to participate. Typically, a startup lays out its project in a whitepaper, including the technical details, the need for the token, how the funds raised will be used, and the overall goals of the project. Once the campaign commences, investors can buy the newly issued tokens with existing digital currencies, often Ethereum or Bitcoin. The allure of ICOs lies in the potential high returns. Early contributors to successful projects like Ethereum or NEO reaped enormous profits. However, the risks are equally significant due to factors like lack of regulation, potential for fraud, and high volatility.

Evaluating ICOs requires a meticulous approach. Start by assessing the credibility of the team behind the project. Research their past experience, their expertise in blockchain technology, and any history of successful projects. The feasibility of the project is another critical area to scrutinize. Understand the technology being proposed and whether it solves a real problem in a way that is achievable and sustainable. Tokenomics, or the economic model of the token, is also vital. Look at the total supply of tokens, the distribution plan, how the tokens will be used within the platform, and what gives the token its value.

Community engagement is an often underestimated aspect of a successful ICO. A strong, active community provides a foundation of support and advocacy for the project. Check social media platforms, Reddit, Telegram, and other forums where project discussions occur. The enthusiasm and engagement level of the community can provide insights into the potential success of the ICO.

Participating in an ICO involves several crucial steps to ensure you do so safely. Conducting thorough due diligence is the first step. This includes reading the project's whitepaper, understanding the legal implications, especially those concerning your jurisdiction, and researching all available information about the project and its team. Once you decide to proceed, you'll need to set up a digital wallet that supports the ICO's token. Make sure it's a wallet for which you control the private keys. Participating directly from an exchange is a common mistake that can lead to you losing your investment.

During the ICO, be vigilant and avoid phishing scams by double-checking all addresses and using official websites only. After acquiring your tokens, the safest practice is to move them to your private wallet, away from exchanges or platforms susceptible to hacks.

Post-ICO strategies involve careful monitoring and management of your investment. Deciding when to hold or sell the tokens can significantly impact your returns. This decision should be based on a thorough market analysis, project updates, and the overall performance of the crypto market. Staying informed through project updates, news sites, and community discussions is crucial. Many projects continue evolving post-ICO, and regulatory changes can also affect your holdings.

Navigating the ICO landscape can be thrilling and potentially rewarding if you are equipped with the proper knowledge and tools. By understanding how ICOs work, evaluating them critically, participating cautiously, and managing your investment wisely, you can engage with this innovative funding mechanism while mitigating the risks involved. Remember, in the volatile world of cryptocurrencies, staying informed and vigilant is your best strategy for success.

Exploring Crypto Derivatives: Options and Futures

Stepping into the realm of cryptocurrency derivatives might sound complex, but it's essentially about strategies that seasoned investors use to optimize their potential gains or hedge against possible losses. Derivatives in the cryptocurrency context involve contracts based on the future value of digital currencies. Two of the most common forms are options and futures. Options allow you to purchase or sell an asset at a predetermined price before a certain expiration date. On the other hand, futures are similar but come with the obligation to purchase or sell that asset at a set price on a specific future date.

Understanding how these instruments work is crucial for anyone looking to dive deeper into the financial mechanics of the crypto world. Trading crypto derivatives involves speculation on the price movements of cryptocurrencies without actually owning them. This is done through contracts that derive their value from the performance of an underlying asset, which, in this case, is a digital currency. The allure of derivatives trading lies in its ability to amplify gains through leverage. This leverage allows traders to gain a larger exposure to the market by using smaller upfront capital, known as margin. However, while leverage can magnify profits, it also increases possible losses, making it a double-edged sword.

Derivative trading platforms like BitMEX, Binance Futures, and Deribit facilitate these transactions. When you engage in a futures contract, for instance, you agree to buy or sell a specific amount of cryptocurrency at a predetermined price on a set future date. The actual mechanics involve various strategies and orders, such as long and short positions, which professional traders use to bet on whether the cryptocurrency will rise or fall. A long position indicates a bet on the price going up, while a short position bets on it going down.

The stakes in derivative trading are high, and so are the risks. The unpredictable nature of cryptocurrencies means prices can swing wildly, impacting derivatives even more due to their leveraged nature. If the market moves against your position, you could lose more than your initial investment, leading to a 'margin call' where you must add more funds to maintain your position or be forced to close it at a loss.

However, the potential rewards can be substantial. Skilled traders use derivatives to hedge other investments or to take advantage of market movements to turn a profit, even in a falling market. For instance, if you hold Bitcoin and think the price will drop temporarily, you might take a short position in Bitcoin futures to profit from this downturn, offsetting the losses in your actual Bitcoin holdings.

Best Practices for Engaging in Crypto Derivatives Trading

Navigating the high-risk world of crypto derivatives requires a well-thought-out strategy and adherence to best practices. First and foremost, educate yourself thoroughly. Understanding the underlying asset, how derivatives work, the specifics of contracts, and the platform you are using is fundamental. Many platforms offer demo accounts where you can practice trading without financial risk, which can be a valuable learning tool.

Choosing a reputable trading platform is crucial. Look for platforms with robust security measures, transparent fee structures, and solid reputations in the community. Since the regulatory landscape for crypto derivatives is still evolving, ensuring that the platform complies with relevant regulations is also essential to protect your investments.

Risk management is another critical area. Use risk management tools and strategies such as stop-loss orders, which automatically sell your contract at a predefined price to prevent significant losses. Diversifying your investments and not pouring all your capital into derivatives trading can also help manage risk.

Continuous learning is part of the journey. The cryptocurrency market is dynamic, with constant developments in technology, regulations, and market conditions. Staying informed through reliable news sources, ongoing education, and active community participation can help you adapt and make better trading decisions.

In conclusion, while the world of crypto derivatives offers exciting opportunities for gaining exposure to cryptocurrencies' price movements without owning them, it comes with high risks that require careful consideration and strategy. Whether you're looking to hedge your existing cryptocurrency holdings or speculate on future prices, understanding the complexities of options and futures is the key to navigating this advanced aspect of crypto investing successfully.

As we wrap up this exploration of advanced investment strategies in the world of cryptocurrency, remember that each instrument and approach we've discussed offers unique opportunities and challenges. From the transformative potential of NFTs and DeFi to the strategic applications of staking and derivatives, the landscape of crypto investing is rich with possibilities. Stay informed, stay cautious, and, as always, make sure your investment decisions align with your financial goals and risk tolerance.

Looking ahead, the next chapter will delve deeper into the evolving regulatory frameworks that shape the global cryptocurrency market, ensuring you're equipped to navigate not only the opportunities but also the complexities of this rapidly changing space.

Chapter 6

Advanced Market Analysis Techniques

Imagine you're a detective in the vast, bustling city of cryptocurrency markets, where every street corner, every shadow, holds clues to potential fortunes and pitfalls. Your tools? It's not just a magnifying glass but a whole arsenal of charts and technical indicators that help you decode the secrets hidden in plain sight. This is the world of technical analysis, a crucial skill for anyone looking to navigate the crypto markets not just with luck but with insight and precision. In this chapter, we'll dive deep into the art and science of reading charts, understanding market behaviors, and making informed predictions that could guide your investment decisions.

Technical Analysis: Reading and Understanding Charts

Chart Types and Setups

In the realm of market analysis, charts are like maps; they don't tell you where to go, but they show you the paths that have been taken before, helping you gauge where you might head next. Understanding different types of charts is foundational in technical analysis. Let's start with the basics: line charts, bar charts, and candlestick charts.

Line charts are the simplest form, plotting the closing price of an asset over a certain period. Imagine drawing a line through the daily closing prices of Bitcoin over a month; what you see is a line chart. It's straightforward and gives you a clear view of how the price has trended over time.

Bar charts take it a notch higher. Each bar represents trading action over a certain period, shows both opening and closing prices, and also the highs and lows. The bottom of the bar shows the lowest traded price for that period, and the top shows the highest price paid. This type of chart provides more data than a line chart and is particularly useful for seeing the volatility during each period.

Candlestick charts, originating from Japan over centuries ago, are arguably the most popular charting method in cryptocurrency trading. Each 'candle' provides four pieces of information: the opening price, the closing price, the high, and the low. What makes candlestick charts particularly valuable are the patterns they form, which traders use to predict price movement. For instance, a series of candles with small bodies but long wicks might suggest a reversal, or a 'doji' candle—where the open and close are virtually the same—can indicate indecision among traders about the asset's value.

Technical Indicators

While charts give you a visual representation of market behavior, technical indicators help by providing mathematical interpretations of market trends and cycles. Some of the most commonly used technical indicators include:

Moving Averages (MA) help smooth out price data by creating a constantly updated average price. The most common are the Simple

Moving Average (SMA) and the Exponential Moving Average (EMA). MAs can help identify a trend's direction and potential reversal points.

The Moving Average Convergence Divergence (MACD) is an indicator of momentum that follows trends and shows the relationship between two moving averages of a cryptocurrency's price. The MACD is calculated by subtracting the 26-period EMA from the 12-period EMA, which results in what is known as the MACD line. A signal line (the 9-period EMA of the MACD line) is plotted on the top of the MACD line and can then function as a trigger for buy and sell indicators.

Relative Strength Index (RSI) measures the speed and change of price movements. RSI oscillates between zero and 100. Traditionally, and according to Wilder, RSI is considered overbought when above 70 and oversold when below 30.

Fibonacci retracement levels are other powerful tools that are particularly interesting because they blend mathematics and art. They are founded on the idea that markets will retrace a foreseeable portion of a move, following which they will continue to move in the original direction. By identifying these retracement levels, you can better predict where the price might find support or resistance.

Chart Patterns and Trends

Recognizing patterns on these charts is like understanding the language of the markets. Some common patterns you should know include:

Head and Shoulders: This pattern, appearing at market tops, suggests a reversal of an uptrend and is one of the most reliable trend reversal patterns.

Flags and Pennants: These are continuation patterns where a sharp price movement is followed by a generally sideways price movement, which is then followed by a continuation of the prior trend.

Wedges: This pattern can signify either a continuance or reversal of a trend, depending on the direction of the wedge.

Integrating Multiple Indicators

The real skill in technical analysis comes not from using a single indicator but from integrating multiple tools to confirm trends and predict movements. For instance, you might use an RSI to identify whether an asset is overbought or oversold, then look for a confirming candlestick pattern and check Fibonacci levels for potential buy or sell points. This multi-layered approach can significantly enhance the reliability of your predictions..

In essence, diving deep into technical analysis equips you with the tools to not only survive in the crypto markets but to thrive. By understanding and utilizing these advanced techniques, you position yourself to make more informed decisions backed not just by gut feeling but by insightful interpretation of market data. As we continue to explore more complex aspects of market analysis in the following sections, keep these foundational tools in mind—they are the building blocks upon which successful trading strategies are built.

Fundamental Analysis of Cryptocurrencies

When you're considering investing in a cryptocurrency, it's like evaluating a tech startup. You wouldn't just look at the price of the company's stock; you'd consider what the company does, how it plans to succeed, and the people behind it. This is where fundamental analysis comes into play, a method extensively used in traditional finance and equally vital in the cryptocurrency world. Fundamental analysis in the context of cryptocurrencies involves assessing the intrinsic value of a digital asset by examining related economic, financial, and other qualitative and quantitative factors.

One of the first aspects to consider is the underlying technology of a cryptocurrency. What problem does this technology solve? How does it improve upon existing solutions? For example, Ethereum introduced smart contracts that automate transactions without any need for intermediaries, which opened up possibilities for numerous applications beyond simple transactions, like decentralized apps (dApps) and decentralized autonomous organizations (DAOs). Evaluating the technology involves understanding the blockchain's protocol, consensus mechanism, scalability, security features, and interoperability with other blockchains. Each of these factors can significantly impact the cryptocurrency's utility and market potential.

The use case of a cryptocurrency is another crucial element. It's essential to identify whether the token has a practical application that can drive demand beyond speculative trading. For instance, Binance Coin (BNB) started as a utility token offering reduced trading fees on the Binance exchange but rapidly expanded its use cases to payments for transaction fees on Binance's chain, token sales, and more. The broader and more robust the use case, the more likely the cryptocurrency will be demanded, which in turn supports its long-term value.

Market potential is about understanding the size of the market or industry the cryptocurrency aims to disrupt or enhance. For example, a cryptocurrency that seeks to streamline cross-border payments in the remittance market, which is worth billions of dollars, may have significant growth potential. Analyzing market potential involves researching the industry size, competitors, and the cryptocurrency's adoption rate within the market.

Importance of the Development Team and Community Support

The team behind a cryptocurrency can be a make-or-break factor in its success. A strong, transparent, and experienced team is often a good indicator of a project's potential. Look into the team members' backgrounds: Have they been involved in other successful projects? Do they have expertise in blockchain and the specific industry the cryptocurrency targets? For example, Vitalik Buterin, co-founder of Ethereum, was already well-known in the cryptocurrency community for his work before launching Ethereum, which helped garner initial support and credibility.

Community support also plays a critical role. Cryptocurrencies with active, engaged communities often see greater innovation and quicker adoption as community members contribute to the development, spread awareness, and use of the cryptocurrency. The size and engagement of the community can often be gauged through social media, cryptocurrency forums, and participation in blockchain events. A vibrant community not only helps in polishing the project through feedback and suggestions but also acts as a vital promotional tool that can drive adoption and increase the cryptocurrency's visibility.

Reading White Papers and Roadmaps

The white paper is a cryptocurrency project's blueprint; it outlines what the project aims to achieve, the technology behind it, the market potential, and more. Reading and critically analyzing a white paper is essential. Look for clarity and feasibility in its objectives, detailed and practical technological explanations, and a clear articulation of the use case. Also, assess the transparency of the white paper: does it cite sources, and does it provide realistic, transparent data to back its claims?

The development roadmap provides insights into the team's long-term vision and their commitment to achieving it. It should outline significant milestones and the timelines for achieving them. Frequent delays, overly ambitious timelines, or a lack of specific targets in the roadmap can be red flags, indicating poor planning or unrealistic goals.

Market and Competitive Analysis

Finally, understanding the competitive landscape is crucial. How does the cryptocurrency stand out from others with similar use cases? Analyzing its competitors involves looking at their market share, technological advantages, and community engagement. For instance, while assessing a new blockchain platform, compare its transaction speed, fees, and scalability to those of direct competitors like Ethereum and Binance Smart Chain.

This competitive analysis not only helps in understanding the strengths and weaknesses of the cryptocurrency you are considering but also in gauging its potential for growth and adoption in comparison to established players. This kind of analysis can provide a more comprehensive view of where the cryptocurrency stands and its potential to secure a niche within the competitive landscape.

By thoroughly applying fundamental analysis, you delve beyond the hype and headlines, equipping yourself with a deep understanding of what drives the value and potential of cryptocurrencies. This methodical approach allows you to make informed decisions, poised to identify opportunities where others might see mere fluctuations.

Sentiment Analysis: Gauging Market Emotions

In the fluctuating universe of cryptocurrency, understanding market sentiment is akin to feeling the pulse of the market. It's about gauging the emotional atmosphere among investors and traders, which can significantly influence price movements. Market sentiment reflects the overall attitude of the marketplace: are people feeling bullish (positive) or bearish (negative) about the future of a particular cryptocurrency? This sentiment can be a powerful yet sometimes elusive, indicator in the volatile crypto markets. Grasping it requires not only keen observation but also the right tools to sift through the vast amounts of data generated by market activities.

Tools and resources for sentiment analysis come in various forms, each offering a distinct slice of the market's emotional pie. Social media analysis, for instance, taps into the pulse of what's being discussed across platforms like Twitter, Reddit, and Facebook. By analyzing the frequency and tone of posts, tweets, and comments, you can get a sense of whether the sentiment towards a cryptocurrency is generally positive, negative, or neutral. Tools like Sentiment Analyzer or CryptoMood use natural language processing and machine learning to quantify this data, providing a more structured and quantifiable measure of social media sentiment.

Opinion polls and sentiment indicators also play crucial roles. Websites like Crypto Fear & Greed Index offer a daily sentiment score by analyzing different sources of data, including volatility, market momentum, and social media. This index, for example, tells you whether investors are feeling excessive fear, which might suggest a potential buying opportunity, or if the market is showing signs of greed, which could indicate a sell-off might be near.

Interpreting News and Media Influence

Understanding how to interpret news and media influence is crucial. The market in cryptocurrency is susceptible to news, which means it often reacts swiftly to announcements related to regulations, technological advancements, or financial results. However, not all news has a lasting impact on market sentiment, and distinguishing impactful news from mere noise is critical.

Impactful news typically involves fundamental changes or significant developments in the cryptocurrency ecosystem, such as a major country announcing new regulatory measures, significant technological breakthroughs, or major financial institutions adopting or investing in cryptocurrency. For example, when a large company like Tesla announced it had invested in Bitcoin and would accept it as payment, the market sentiment soared, driving up Bitcoin's price significantly.

On the other hand, the daily fluctuations of opinions and minor updates that don't affect the core aspects of a cryptocurrency might create noise—temporary ripples that might seem important but generally don't lead to long-term impact. Learning to differentiate between these can help you avoid reactionary decisions based on transient emotions and focus on news that substantiates potential long-term shifts in market dynamics.

Applying Sentiment Analysis

Incorporating sentiment analysis into your overall trading strategy can significantly enhance your decision-making process. It's about merging the emotional pulse of the market with more traditional technical and fundamental analyses to form a comprehensive view of the potential market movements.

For instance, if your technical analysis suggests that a cryptocurrency is about to break out, but sentiment analysis shows extreme fear in the market, it might be wise to tread cautiously. The market could be reacting to a recent piece of negative news, and despite what the technical indicators suggest, the price might drop instead of climb.

Using real-world examples, consider the impact of China's announcements on cryptocurrency regulations. Each time there was news about China tightening its stance on cryptocurrencies, the market typically reacted negatively, often resulting in significant price drops. Traders using sentiment analysis would have been on alert for such news and could have adjusted their trading strategies accordingly, potentially limiting losses or capitalizing on the buy-back opportunities these dips often present.

In essence, sentiment analysis offers a way to harness the emotional undercurrents of the market, providing you with insights that can help you anticipate and react to price changes more effectively. It's about adding another layer to your investment strategy, one that considers not just the numbers and trends but also the human emotions that drive market movements. By mastering this analysis, you position yourself to navigate the crypto markets not just with information but with insight into the collective mood of the market participants.

Leveraging Trading Bots: Do's and Don'ts

Imagine you had a tool that could handle the rapid and often exhausting demands of cryptocurrency trading for you, executing trades at optimal times, day or night, without your constant supervision. That's precisely what trading bots are designed to do. In essence, trading bots are software programs that will connect to a cryptocurrency exchange and make trades on your behalf based on predefined conditions. These bots can analyze market data, interpret it according to your strategy, and even make trading decisions that help maximize your profits—all without any direct input from you once they are set up.

When selecting a trading bot, several crucial factors come into play. Reliability is paramount; a bot that frequently goes offline or has software bugs can result in missed trading opportunities or even losses. Security is another primary consideration; the bot should have robust security measures to protect your investment, especially since it will have access to your exchange account. The user interface should be intuitive and user-friendly, allowing you to configure settings and understand features without needing a deep background in technology or trading. Lastly, cost is an important factor; some bots come with a subscription fee, while others might take a percentage of your profits.

Additionally, a solid community support system can be invaluable. A vibrant community can provide practical insights, strategies, and feedback that can help you get the most out of your trading bot. Developers who are transparent about their practices and offer regular updates can also be a sign of a trustworthy product.

Setting up a trading bot involves several steps, each important to ensure the bot functions correctly and aligns with your trading strategy. Initially, you need to choose a bot that fits your trading needs and is compatible with your chosen cryptocurrency exchange. Once selected, you'll typically download and install the software. Configuring your bot is the next critical step. This involves setting up trading strategies—the instructions that the bot follows when buying and selling on your behalf. These might include when to enter and exit trades, risk management rules, and what portion of your portfolio to trade. Many advanced bots offer backtesting features, which will allow you to test your strategy against historical market data before putting real money on the line. This can help refine your plan without any risk.

However, while trading bots can offer significant advantages, they also come with their own set of risks and ethical considerations. One of the primary concerns is market manipulation. Some unscrupulous traders might use bots to engage in practices like wash trading or pump-and-dump schemes, which are illegal and harmful to the market. It's crucial to use bots responsibly and ensure that your trading strategies don't inadvertently contribute to manipulative practices. Another risk is over-reliance on bots. Relying too heavily on automated systems can make you complacent about the nuances of the market and detached from your own trading decisions. It's essential to remain engaged and monitor your bot's performance, adjusting strategies as market conditions change.

In conclusion, when used wisely, trading bots can be powerful tools for automating trading strategies and maximizing your trading efficiency. By understanding and managing their associated risks and maintaining an active role in managing your strategies, you can leverage trading bots effectively while safeguarding your investments.

Cryptocurrency and Global Economic Indicators

In the interconnected world of finance, the waves of global economic indicators not only ripple through traditional markets such as commodities and stocks but also wash over the shores of the cryptocurrency landscape. Understanding how elements such as inflation rates, exchange rates, and economic policies influence cryptocurrency markets can offer you a nuanced perspective, enhancing your ability to make informed investment decisions.

Let's consider inflation rates, which reflect the rate at which the general level of prices for goods and services is rising and, subsequently, purchasing power is falling. Central banks attempt to limit inflation and avoid deflation in order to keep the economy running smoothly. Consider how Bitcoin has often been referred to as "digital gold," a potential hedge against inflation. This comparison stems from the cryptocurrency's designed scarcity, as there will only ever be 21 million bitcoins. When traditional currencies face inflation, meaning each unit of currency will purchase fewer goods and services, this scarcity can make Bitcoin more attractive, potentially driving up its price. Observing how cryptocurrencies react in countries experiencing high inflation rates can provide insights into future movements.

Exchange rates, the value of one currency for the purpose of conversion to another, also play a significant role. For instance, if the U.S. dollar strengthens against other currencies, it can make dollar-priced assets, including cryptocurrencies, more expensive for foreign investors, potentially reducing demand. Conversely, if the dollar weakens, those same assets become cheaper and more attractive to foreign investors, possibly pushing demand higher. Monitoring these trends can help predict inflows and outflows of capital into cryptocurrencies from abroad, offering strategic investment insights.

Furthermore, economic policies, particularly those related to monetary policy, can significantly impact cryptocurrency markets. Policies that increase money supply, typically lowering interest rates, can lead to lower returns on savings denominated in those currencies. This might make higher-risk assets, like cryptocurrencies, more appealing. Conversely, tightening monetary policies might make traditional investments more attractive, potentially decreasing investment in crypto assets. Understanding these relationships and their indicators can guide your crypto investment timing and strategy.

Cryptocurrencies as Economic Indicators

Interestingly, cryptocurrencies themselves are beginning to be viewed as economic indicators. Consider the relationship between Bitcoin prices and geopolitical tensions or economic instability. Often, in times of economic uncertainty, there's an observable increase in Bitcoin trading volumes and price, suggesting that some view and use cryptocurrencies as digital safe havens. Analyzing these movements can offer you insights into global economic sentiments and trends, further illustrating the intricate ties between traditional economic indicators and the relatively new crypto markets.

Correlation with Traditional Markets

Exploring the correlation between cryptocurrencies and traditional financial markets, such as stocks and commodities, can reveal fascinating insights into investor behavior and risk appetite. Historically, cryptocurrencies like Bitcoin have shown periods of both correlation and non-correlation with traditional markets. For instance, during times of market stress, such as the early months of the COVID-19 pandemic, both Bitcoin and stock markets saw significant drops, suggesting a temporary correlation likely due to investors seeking liquidity. However, there are also periods where cryptocurrencies have moved independently of traditional markets, highlighting their potential as diversification tools. Understanding these correlations and their exceptions can help in crafting a diversified investment portfolio that can better withstand market volatility.

Strategic Planning Using Economic Indicators

Incorporating global economic indicators into your cryptocurrency investment strategy involves scenario planning and hedging techniques. Scenario planning allows you to prepare for different future economic conditions, adjusting your investment strategy accordingly. For example, if you anticipate an economic downturn, you might increase your holdings in cryptocurrencies that have historically performed well as safe-haven assets. On the other hand, by hedging, using financial instruments or market strategies, you can offset the risk of adverse price movements, which is crucial. You might hedge your crypto investments by keeping a portion of your portfolio in fiat currencies or traditional assets like gold, which might behave differently under various economic scenarios.

By weaving these strategies into your investment approach, you can more adeptly navigate the complex interplay between global economic indicators and cryptocurrency markets. This not only enhances your ability to adapt to changing conditions but also positions you to capitalize on opportunities that others might miss.

As this chapter concludes, remember that the dance between cryptocurrencies and global economic indicators is nuanced and complex. By understanding this relationship, you're better equipped to make informed decisions, potentially leading to more robust investment outcomes. As we transition into the next chapter, we'll explore the regulatory frameworks shaping the global cryptocurrency landscape, an understanding of which is essential for every informed investor.

Chapter 7

The Intersection of Cryptocurrency and Technology

Imagine stepping into a world where your health records are as secure as the vaults of a bank, where every pill you take can be traced back to its origin, and where medical bureaucracy doesn't slow down the speed at which you receive care. This isn't a far-off fantasy; it's a reality being forged at the intersection of cryptocurrency and modern technology, particularly through the use of blockchain. In this chapter, we'll delve into how blockchain is revolutionizing the healthcare sector, enhancing data privacy, streamlining processes, and ensuring the authenticity of pharmaceuticals.

Blockchain in Healthcare: Improving Data Privacy

Securing Patient Data

In the realm of healthcare, patient data is both invaluable and incredibly sensitive. The security of this data is paramount, not just to maintain privacy but also to ensure trust in the healthcare system. Blockchain technology offers a potent solution by creating tamper-proof records of patient data. When information is added to a blockchain, it is encrypted and distributed across a network of computers, thereby making it nearly impossible to alter. Each block of data is linked to the one before it and after it, creating a chronological chain of records that is viewable by all parties but can only be updated through consensus among participants in the network.

This level of security means that sensitive information like your medical history, treatment plans, and prescription details are protected from unauthorized access and fraud. For you, this translates into peace of mind knowing your medical records are secure and only accessible to healthcare providers who have explicit permission to view them. Moreover, blockchain enables the secure sharing of your health data among authorized parties. Whether it's for consultation, diagnosis, or treatment, healthcare providers can access up-to-date, accurate information from anywhere in the world, facilitating better and faster care.

Streamlining Processes

The healthcare industry is notoriously bogged down by complex administrative processes, which can delay the delivery of care and lead to increased costs. Blockchain technology can streamline these processes by automating administrative tasks such as billing, claims processing, and compliance management. Smart contracts, which are self-executing contracts with the terms directly written into code, can automatically verify and process claims based on pre-set rules, significantly reducing the time and cost associated with manual processing.

For example, a blockchain system can automatically verify if a particular medical procedure is covered under a patient's insurance policy and then instantly process the claim, reducing the need for back-and-forth paperwork. This not only speeds up the processing of claims but also reduces the likelihood of errors and fraud, ensuring that healthcare providers are paid promptly and accurately for their services.

Enhancing Drug Traceability

The selling of counterfeit drugs is a significant issue in the pharmaceutical industry, posing serious risks to patient safety and costing the industry billions each year. Fortunately,   provides a robust solution to this problem through enhanced traceability of drug supply chains. Each step of a drug's journey from manufacturing to delivery can be recorded on a blockchain, creating a permanent history of the product's movement that can easily be traced back to its source.

This level of traceability ensures that you can be confident in the safety and authenticity of the medications you take. It also allows pharmaceutical companies to quickly trace and recall defective products, minimizing the impact of potential health risks.

Case Studies

Several healthcare organizations have already started to harness the power of blockchain to enhance data privacy and operational efficiency. For instance, a major hospital in the United States implemented a blockchain-based system to secure patient records and manage consent forms. The system allowed the hospital to easily manage and retrieve consent documents, ensuring compliance with healthcare regulations while providing patients with greater control over their personal information.

Another example is a global pharmaceutical company that used blockchain to track the distribution of medication in real time across multiple countries. This system helped the company combat counterfeiting and ensure that patients received genuine products.

These case studies demonstrate not only the practical applications of blockchain in healthcare but also its potential to fundamentally transform the industry, making it more secure, efficient, and patient-focused. As we continue to explore the intersection of cryptocurrency and technology, it becomes clear that the implications are vast, and the potential for positive change is enormous.

Smart Contracts: Transforming Legal and Business Processes

Smart contracts might sound high-tech and complex, but at their core, they're merely programs stored on a blockchain that run when predetermined conditions are met. They are digital contracts that automatically execute, control, or document legally relevant events and actions according to the terms agreed upon by the parties involved. Picture this: you're buying a house, and instead of going through heaps of paperwork, waiting for approvals, and dealing with intermediaries, you use a smart contract. This contract could automatically ensure that when you transfer the payment, the digital title deed is transferred to you. No middlemen, no extra fees, and no delays.

The advantages of smart contracts extend beyond just making transactions quicker. They can drastically reduce transaction costs because they cut out middlemen like brokers and lawyers, whose services can be costly. Additionally, smart contracts are executed by the computer code itself, which can dramatically reduce any errors that can arise from manually filling out heaps of forms. Also, because records on blockchains are encrypted, they are highly secure. The transparency of having transactions recorded on a blockchain ensures that all parties can view contract changes and outcomes, reducing the potential for disputes and enhancing trust among parties.

Looking beyond cryptocurrencies, smart contracts have diverse applications across various industries, reshaping how businesses and legal processes are handled. For example, in real estate, smart contracts may be used to handle the transfer of property titles and automate payments, reducing the time and paperwork involved in real estate transactions. In supply chain management, these contracts can be used to track the production, shipment, and delivery of products in real time. They ensure that each step in the supply chain is recorded, and if a product fails to reach a checkpoint by a specific time, the contract can trigger alerts and even withhold payments until issues are resolved.

In the realm of intellectual property rights, smart contracts can automate royalty payments. For instance, every time a song is downloaded, or a book is purchased online, a smart contract can ensure that the artists or authors receive their royalties immediately. This not only ensures that artists are paid fairly but also speeds up the process that customarily involves a lot of paperwork and time.

However, while smart contracts offer numerous benefits, they are not without challenges. One of the main hurdles is the legal recognition of smart contracts as legitimate substitutes for traditional contracts. The law in many areas is still catching up with the technology, and in many jurisdictions, digital contracts are not yet recognized as legally binding. This poses a risk, especially in transactions involving large sums of money or significant assets.

Scalability is another issue. As more transactions are carried out on blockchain networks, the volume of data being processed can lead to congestion, slowing down transactions and increasing costs, which diminishes one of the fundamental advantages of using smart contracts. Furthermore, while smart contracts are secure, they are only as good as the code they are written with, as bugs in the code can lead to unintended consequences, including security vulnerabilities. These technical obstacles require ongoing attention and improvements in blockchain and smart contract technologies.

Despite these challenges, the potential of smart contracts to revolutionize legal and business processes is immense. As technology advances and more sectors recognize and adapt to these benefits, we can see a significant transformation in how contracts are executed and enforced. This could lead to a more efficient, transparent, and fair way of conducting transactions across many aspects of business and law.

The Impact of Cryptocurrency on Global Remittances

Reducing Transfer Costs

Imagine sending money to your family halfway across the world, and more of your hard-earned cash actually reaches them without being eaten up by hefty transaction fees. That's one of the transformative benefits cryptocurrencies bring to the table, especially in the context of global remittances. Traditional wire transfers and international banking typically involve multiple intermediaries, each taking a slice of the transaction as processing fees. Cryptocurrencies streamline this process by enabling direct peer-to-peer transactions without the need for these intermediaries, significantly reducing the costs involved.

This reduction in cost is not just marginal; it can mean the difference between a family in a developing country affording an extra week's worth of groceries or not. For instance, consider a typical bank transfer where transaction fees can range anywhere from 5% to as high as 20% of the amount being sent, depending on the countries involved. In contrast, the transaction fee for sending cryptocurrencies like Bitcoin or Ethereum might only be a few cents or a small percentage, regardless of the amount or the geographic locations of the sender and recipient.

The impact is profound in regions where a significant portion of the population relies on remittances from family members working abroad. Lower fees mean more money sent home can be spent on essential living expenses, education, or starting small businesses, potentially lifting communities out of poverty and stimulating local economies.

Increasing Speed and Accessibility

Beyond just reducing costs, cryptocurrencies can revolutionize how quickly money is transferred across borders. Traditional remittance pathways can be slow, sometimes requiring several days to process due to the checks and balances of intermediate banks and financial services. Cryptocurrencies operate on blockchain technology that allows for almost instantaneous transactions. This means that what used to take days can now happen in a matter of minutes or even seconds, regardless of where the sender and recipient are located.

This speed of transaction provides not just convenience but also security. The quicker the money is transferred, the less time there is for potential interference or fraud along the way. Moreover, the accessibility of cryptocurrencies is a game-changer for the unbanked or underbanked populations. A significant number of adults worldwide do not have access to traditional banking services, which excludes them from the global financial system and makes it particularly challenging and expensive to receive remittances through conventional means.

Cryptocurrencies can be accessed by anyone with a smartphone and an internet connection, both of which are increasingly widespread, even in developing countries. This accessibility means that remittances can reach more people directly and safely, contributing to financial inclusion and empowerment.

Risks and Regulatory Challenges

However, the use of cryptocurrencies in remittances is not without its challenges, as the instability of cryptocurrency prices can be a substantial risk. The value of cryptocurrencies can dramatically increase or decrease within a short period, which means the actual value received by the end recipient can vary unpredictably. This risk can be mitigated by converting cryptocurrencies to stablecoins—cryptocurrencies pegged to less volatile assets like the US dollar—or immediately converting the received cryptocurrency into local currency.

Regulatory uncertainty also poses a challenge. A cryptocurrency's legal status varies significantly from one country to another. In some places, it is still a grey area with ongoing debates about how to implement effective regulations without stifling innovation. These regulatory challenges can impact the legality and reliability of using cryptocurrencies for remittances. Staying informed about the regulatory environment and compliance requirements in both the sender's and recipient's countries is crucial for those considering cryptocurrencies for remittances.

Examples of Cryptocurrency Use in Remittances

Several countries and entities have successfully harnessed the power of cryptocurrencies to enhance their remittance systems. For example, in the Philippines, a country where remittances constitute a significant part of the GDP, several blockchain-based remittance services have emerged. These services leverage cryptocurrencies to facilitate faster and cheaper transfers for the millions of Filipinos working abroad. In Africa, companies like BitPesa use blockchain technology to help businesses in multiple countries pay their employees and suppliers in other parts of the world, reducing transfer costs and times dramatically.

These examples underscore the potential of cryptocurrencies to transform the remittance industry by making transfers faster, cheaper, and more accessible. As technology continues to evolve and regulatory frameworks become clearer, the role of cryptocurrencies in remittances is likely to grow, offering a lifeline to millions of individuals who depend on these funds for their livelihood.

Cryptocurrencies in the Gaming Industry

In the dynamic world of gaming, where fantasy realms and digital landscapes flourish, cryptocurrencies are making significant inroads, transforming how transactions are conducted and how players interact with virtual economies. Think of a gaming world where every purchase of armor or every trade of goods doesn't just rely on traditional in-game currency that holds no value outside the game but uses cryptocurrencies that carry real-world value. This integration not only enhances the gaming experience by adding a layer of authenticity and value to in-game economies but also revolutionizes the financial dynamics of gaming.

Cryptocurrencies facilitate transactions within these virtual worlds with a level of efficiency and security that traditional in-game currencies simply cannot match. By using blockchain technology, transactions are recorded on a decentralized ledger, ensuring transparency and reducing the chances of fraud. This setup allows for the seamless purchase of digital goods and services within the game, making the process smoother and more reliable. For gamers, this means the ability to buy, sell, and trade in-game assets without the usual hassles of conversion rates and transaction fees associated with standard currencies. It connects different gaming platforms and economies, making digital assets more liquid and, thus, more valuable.

Moreover, cryptocurrencies are dramatically changing how players interact with their virtual assets. Through blockchain technology, when you acquire an in-game item, it can actually be yours. This means that players have absolute ownership of their in-game assets, as each item can be uniquely identified and ownership verified on the blockchain. This ownership extends beyond the game itself, allowing players to trade or sell their assets on external markets, potentially earning real money. The implications are profound; items like unique swords, rare skins, or even characters can become collectibles, much like physical items in the real world. This shift not only makes gaming more engaging and potentially profitable for players but also ensures that their investments in time and money are tangible and protected.

For game developers, cryptocurrencies open up new avenues for monetization that go beyond traditional methods like advertisements or one-time in-app purchases. Through tokenization, where in-game assets are linked to crypto tokens, developers can create more immersive and financially sustainable ecosystems. Players might buy tokens to access special content or unique abilities, and because these tokens can also be traded outside the game, they remain valuable to players, driving engagement and retention. Additionally, developers can earn a commission on transactions happening in and out of the game, providing a continuous revenue stream that is not limited to initial sales or ads.

While the potential of cryptocurrencies in gaming is vast, integrating them into mainstream gaming platforms presents several challenges. Scalability is a major concern; as games attract millions of players worldwide, the underlying blockchain must be able to handle a vast number of transactions quickly and efficiently. Current technology still struggles with these demands, leading to potential delays and increased transaction costs, which could detract from the gaming experience.

User adoption also poses a significant hurdle. Despite the growing popularity of cryptocurrencies, many gamers are new to blockchain technology and may hesitate to embrace these new systems. Educating users and demonstrating the tangible benefits of using cryptocurrencies in gaming are crucial steps toward widespread adoption.

Speculating on future developments, as gaming platforms become more sophisticated and blockchain technology advances, the integration of cryptocurrencies in gaming could become more seamless. Innovations such as layer-two solutions or sidechains could address the issues of scalability by allowing transactions to occur off the main blockchain, speeding up processing times and reducing costs. As more gamers recognize the benefits of actual digital ownership and developers find innovative ways to incorporate token economies, cryptocurrencies could well become a standard element of the gaming industry, transforming how players and developers interact and creating a new paradigm for the digital gaming economy.

Blockchain for Social Good: Real-World Applications

When you think of blockchain, your mind might first jump to cryptocurrencies and financial transactions. However, the potential of blockchain extends far beyond this, playing a pivotal role in social change across the globe. One of the most significant impacts of blockchain is its capability to enhance trust and transparency, particularly within charitable organizations. Traditionally, when you donate to a charity, it can be challenging to track where your money actually goes or whether it's being used effectively. Blockchain introduces a layer of accountability and transparency that was previously difficult to achieve.

On a blockchain, every transaction is recorded on a public ledger, which is immutable. This means that once a record is made, it cannot be altered or deleted. For charitable organizations, this can revolutionize how donations are tracked and reported. Donors can see exactly where their funds are going and follow the money as it moves toward its intended projects. This transparency not only reassures donors but also discourages mismanagement of funds within the organizations. For example, a blockchain platform could be used to track the distribution of funds in real-time as they are passed from the charity to purchase supplies and then to their final destination in a relief effort. This kind of traceability can significantly boost the trust and credibility of charitable organizations, encouraging more people to donate and contribute to crucial causes.

Blockchain also holds transformative potential for empowering economically disadvantaged communities. One significant way it achieves this is through the provision of secure digital identities. Around the world, a shocking number of people do not have any form of official identification, which can prevent them from accessing essential services like banking, healthcare, and education. Blockchain technology can offer a secure, immutable form of digital ID that is recognized and accepted worldwide. With such an ID, individuals can open bank accounts, sign legal contracts, access government services, and more. Moreover, blockchain can facilitate microloans directly to individuals or small businesses, bypassing traditional banking barriers and high interest rates. This direct financial empowerment can be a game-changer for lifting communities out of poverty.

In terms of enhancing environmental sustainability, blockchain technology is being used innovatively to support efforts across the globe. One notable application is in the tracking of carbon credits. Carbon credits are permits that allow the holder to emit a certain amount of carbon dioxide or other greenhouse gases. The calculation, tracking, and exchange of these credits can be complex and opaque. Blockchain provides a tamper-proof, transparent system for managing carbon credits to ensure that they are only counted once and used correctly. Additionally, blockchain is being utilized to verify the sustainability of supply chains. For instance, it can track the journey of a product from a sustainably managed forest through processing and manufacturing all the way to the retail shelf. This not only helps to ensure compliance with environmental standards but also boosts consumer confidence in sustainable products.

Case Studies of Successful Implementations

Looking at real-world examples, the World Food Programme (WFP) has successfully implemented blockchain technology to aid in the distribution of assistance to refugees. Their 'Building Blocks' project uses blockchain to make cash transfers more efficient, secure, and transparent. This initiative has helped to significantly reduce payment costs, increase data security, and ensure that aid reaches its intended recipients without any diversion.

Another compelling case is that of BitGive, the first Bitcoin nonprofit recognized by the IRS. BitGive has developed a platform called GiveTrack, which uses blockchain to allow donors to trace their donations. Donors can track how funds are spent, see the outcomes of their donations, and even communicate with the beneficiaries. This level of transparency and engagement increases the trust and satisfaction of donors, potentially leading to more substantial and sustained contributions.

These cases highlight just a few ways blockchain is being used to foster transparency, empower individuals, and address complex environmental issues. By leveraging this technology, we can make significant strides toward a more equitable and sustainable world. As we continue to explore the vast potential of blockchain, it becomes increasingly clear that its impact extends well beyond the financial sector, offering promising solutions to some of the most pressing social challenges of our time.

Chapter 8

Cryptocurrency and Society

Imagine a world where your economic status or geographical location doesn't limit your access to financial resources. Where the simple click of a button could offer you the same financial services that someone in a bustling financial district enjoys. Cryptocurrency is not just digital money; it's a revolutionary tool that is leveling the financial playing field across the globe. Let's delve into understanding its pivotal role in enhancing financial inclusion, particularly for those previously sidelined by traditional banking systems.

The Role of Cryptocurrency in Financial Inclusion

Cryptocurrency emerges as a beacon of hope, especially for the unbanked and underbanked populations. Think about someone living in a remote village where the nearest bank could be miles away, requiring hours of travel. For such an individual, traditional banking isn't just inconvenient; it's practically inaccessible. Cryptocurrencies are changing this narrative by providing financial services through mobile phones—a technology increasingly widespread even in remote areas. This aspect of digital currencies is not just about convenience but about offering fundamental financial services: saving money, receiving loans, and ensuring direct payments for work, which are crucial for daily survival and economic advancement.

The barriers to entry in the traditional banking world—documentation requirements, minimum balance stipulations, and sometimes discriminatory practices—often exclude low-income individuals and those without a fixed address. Cryptocurrencies dismantle these barriers. They operate on technology that allows anyone with a smartphone and internet access to create a wallet without any minimum balance or the bureaucratic red tape associated with traditional bank accounts. This inclusivity opens a world of opportunities for millions who were previously part of the cash-only economy, susceptible to theft and loss.

Empowering Microtransactions and Microfinance

One of the most transformative aspects regarding emerging markets of cryptocurrencies is their ability to facilitate microtransactions and microfinance. These are crucial for small-scale entrepreneurs who might need small amounts of capital to start or expand their businesses but are unable to secure loans from traditional banks due to a lack of collateral or credit history. Cryptocurrencies enable transactions that are not just secure and fast but also incredibly low in cost, allowing for the profitable transfer of tiny amounts of money. This capability is vital for microentrepreneurs looking to grow their businesses one small step at a time.

Moreover, the divisibility and portability of cryptocurrencies mean that these transactions can occur anywhere, eliminating the geographical constraints that often hinder traditional banking. A craftsman in a small village can receive a microloan from a lender in a metropolitan city, or a farmer can buy seeds using a fraction of a Bitcoin or Ethereum without needing physical cash or going through a bank.

Case Studies of Cryptocurrency in Emerging Markets

Let's consider a few real-world implementations that highlight the impact of cryptocurrencies on financial inclusion. In Kenya, the introduction of BitPesa has allowed users to send and receive money across borders more cheaply and quickly than traditional banks would allow. BitPesa uses Bitcoin as a medium for transferring funds, significantly lowering the cost of transactions and enabling East Africans to do business with companies around the world without needing a bank account.

In Venezuela, amidst hyperinflation and economic instability, cryptocurrencies have provided an alternative means of storing value that's more stable than the local currency. Platforms like Dash have become popular because they offer not only an opportunity for savings but also for transactions, allowing users to pay for daily expenses such as groceries and medicine with cryptocurrency. This shift has been crucial in helping individuals and businesses survive in an economy where the national currency has failed.

These examples underscore the profound impact cryptocurrencies are having on financial inclusion, demonstrating their potential to empower economically marginalized communities. By providing an alternative to traditional monetary systems, cryptocurrencies are not just changing how people transact; they are fundamentally altering the economic landscape, offering more people the opportunity to participate in the global economy on fairer terms. As we continue to explore the intersection of cryptocurrency and society, it's clear that the potential of these digital assets extends far beyond mere financial speculation; they are powerful tools for social and economic empowerment, paving the way for a more inclusive global financial system.

Privacy and Anonymity in Cryptocurrencies

When you think about privacy in financial transactions, what comes to mind might be a sealed envelope or a private meeting room. In the digital world, achieving this level of confidentiality is complex, especially with traditional financial systems that inherently require some level of personal disclosure. Enter privacy-focused cryptocurrencies like Monero and Zcash, which provide a digital equivalent of that sealed envelope, ensuring that your financial transactions remain confidential and untraceable. These cryptocurrencies use sophisticated cryptographic techniques to shield transaction details, including the identity of the sender and receiver, as well as the amount being transferred, from being publicly accessible on the blockchain.

Monero, for example, utilizes something called ring signatures and stealth addresses. Ring signatures mix a user's account keys with public keys from the blockchain to create a unique signature that can authenticate a transaction without revealing which specific keys were involved. This mechanism makes it extraordinarily difficult to trace the transaction back to any user. A stealth address adds another layer of privacy by creating a one-time address for each transaction so that all payments are received from unique addresses that cannot be linked to any previous transactions or to the receiver's primary address. Zcash uses a different approach known as zk-SNARKs (Zero-Knowledge Succinct Non-Interactive Arguments of Knowledge), which allows transactions to be verified without revealing any details about the transaction to the blockchain. This technology essentially allows for a transaction to be fully encrypted on the blockchain yet still considered valid and secure.

While these privacy features offer significant advantages for users seeking anonymity, they also bring forth complex legal and ethical considerations. Privacy coins are often scrutinized because their anonymity can potentially be exploited for illegal activities, including tax evasion, money laundering, and financing terrorism. This has led to debates about the balance between privacy rights and regulatory requirements. Regulatory bodies in several countries are grappling with creating frameworks that prevent illicit use without infringing on individual privacy rights. The challenge lies in implementing know-your-customer (KYC) and anti-money laundering (AML) laws in a way that does not completely strip away the anonymity features that define privacy coins.

Compared to traditional financial systems, where every transaction through a bank or credit card is traceable and tied to personal identities, cryptocurrencies offer a distinct advantage in terms of privacy. Traditional systems often involve extensive personal documentation and continuous tracking of financial activities, leaving a digital paper trail that is accessible to banks and, by extension, to government bodies. In contrast, transactions with privacy coins can occur without any personal information being disclosed, giving users control over their own financial privacy.

However, it's crucial to address common challenges and misconceptions associated with these cryptocurrencies. A significant challenge is the misconception that privacy in cryptocurrencies is absolute. While privacy coins enhance anonymity, they are not entirely untraceable. Advanced blockchain analysis techniques and network surveillance can sometimes lead to the de-anonymization of parties involved in transactions, especially if other operational security measures are not effectively implemented by the users.

Moreover, the misconception that privacy coins are primarily used for illicit activities can overshadow their legitimate uses, such as protecting individuals living under oppressive regimes or safeguarding sensitive transactions in business dealings.

Understanding the nuances of privacy in cryptocurrencies involves recognizing what these technologies can and cannot do. While they offer enhanced privacy compared to traditional financial transactions, they are not a foolproof solution to all privacy concerns. As the technology evolves and regulatory landscapes adjust, the conversation around privacy coins will likely continue to grow, highlighting the ongoing need to balance privacy rights with security and regulatory requirements.

The Environmental Impact of Cryptocurrency Mining

When you hear about cryptocurrency mining, you might imagine complex algorithms and digital coins popping out of the ether. However, the real picture involves massive computational power and, consequently, significant energy consumption, especially for cryptocurrencies that operate on a proof-of-work (PoW) system. PoW, used by Bitcoin and many other cryptocurrencies, requires miners to solve complex mathematical problems to validate transactions and secure the network. This process, known as mining, is energy-intensive because it involves numerous computers competing to solve these problems first, thereby earning the right to add a new transaction block to the blockchain.

The energy consumption of these mining operations is staggering. For instance, Bitcoin's annual energy consumption is comparable to that of entire countries like Sweden or Malaysia. This immense energy use primarily stems from the electricity needed to power the high-performance computers that miners use. Much of this energy comes from power plants that burn fossil fuels, which contributes significantly to carbon emissions, a leading cause of global warming. Moreover, the electronic waste produced by cryptocurrency mining is a growing concern. As mining hardware becomes obsolete, it creates a stream of electronic waste that is difficult to recycle, given the specialized nature of these devices.

Beyond the carbon footprint, large-scale mining operations can also have more direct impacts on the environment. In regions where cryptocurrency mining is prevalent, the demand for electricity can lead to increased strain on local power grids, which can cause power shortages and increase the reliance on environmentally harmful backup power sources like diesel generators. Additionally, the heat generated by extensive mining farms can contribute to local temperature increases, affecting local climates and wildlife.

Despite these challenges, the cryptocurrency community is increasingly aware of the environmental impacts and is taking steps toward more sustainable practices. Innovations and initiatives aimed at reducing the environmental footprint of cryptocurrency mining are on the rise. One significant shift is the move towards using renewable energy sources to power mining operations. Solar, wind, and hydroelectric power are becoming more popular among miners, especially in regions where these resources are abundant and cheap. For example, some mining farms in Scandinavia take advantage of cheap hydroelectric power and a cool climate to reduce the energy consumption and cooling needs of mining operations.

Another promising development is the shift towards less energy-intensive consensus algorithms like proof-of-stake (PoS). Unlike PoW, PoS does not necessitate miners to solve intricate mathematical problems. Instead, validators are selected to create new blocks based on the number of coins they hold and are willing to use as collateral. This method not only reduces the amount of power needed to maintain the network but also incentivizes the holding of coins, which can lead to a more stable cryptocurrency environment. Ethereum is the second-largest cryptocurrency by market capitalization and is in the process of transitioning from PoW to PoS. This move is expected to decrease its energy consumption by up to 99%.

Globally, the regulatory response to the environmental impact of cryptocurrency mining has been varied. Some countries have embraced the challenge, implementing regulations and providing incentives for cleaner mining practices. For instance, Iceland has become a hub for sustainable cryptocurrency mining due to its abundance of renewable energy sources and natural cooling environments. Meanwhile, other countries have taken a more stringent approach. China, once home to over two-thirds of the world's cryptocurrency mining, has banned the practice entirely in some regions, citing excessive energy consumption and environmental concerns.

These examples illustrate the complex interplay between innovation, regulation, and environmental responsibility in the realm of cryptocurrency mining. As the industry continues to evolve, the push for sustainable development could not only alleviate the environmental impact of digital currencies but also lead to broader applications of eco-friendly technology in other sectors. By staying informed and supporting sustainable practices, you can contribute to this vital transition, ensuring that the future of finance does not come at the expense of the planet's health.

Cryptocurrency and Cybersecurity: What You Need to Know

Navigating the digital seas of cryptocurrency not only offers vast opportunities but also brings its own set of risks, particularly in cybersecurity. As you dive deeper into this world, understanding these risks and knowing how to protect yourself are crucial.

Common threats like exchange hacks, wallet breaches, and phishing attacks can turn what should be an exciting venture into a nightmare. Imagine logging in to find your digital wallet has been emptied or your personal information has been compromised. These scenarios are not just hypothetical; they happen more often than you might think.

Exchange hacks have been some of the most high-profile security breaches, with attackers stealing millions of dollars worth of cryptocurrencies. These platforms are prime targets due to the large amounts of assets they hold. Similarly, wallet breaches occur when unauthorized users gain access to a cryptocurrency wallet, enabling them to transfer funds. Often, this can be due to weak security practices like the use of simple passwords or storing information in easily accessible places. Phishing attacks, perhaps the most insidious, involve tricking individuals into giving away sensitive information, such as login credentials or private keys, often through fake websites or misleading emails that appear to be from legitimate sources.

Preventing such incidents begins with adhering to best practices for security. One of the most effective measures you can take is the use of hardware wallets to store your cryptocurrencies. Think of a hardware wallet as a personal safe—only much more compact and portable. Unlike online wallets or those hosted on mobile devices or computers, hardware wallets store your private keys offline on a physical device that can resemble a USB stick. This method, known as 'cold storage,' significantly reduces the risk of your funds being accessed via the Internet. Additionally, maintaining robust security on your physical device is crucial; this includes setting up strong, unique passwords and considering additional security measures like biometric locks.

Moreover, multi-factor authentication (MFA) adds an extra layer of security, but bear in mind that MFA requires more than one method of verification before access is granted; typically, it is something you know (like a password), something you have (like a smartphone to receive a code), and something you are (like a fingerprint or facial recognition). Implementing MFA can make unauthorized access considerably more difficult, providing an additional safeguard against hacking attempts.

The inherent features of blockchain technology also contribute significantly to enhancing cybersecurity. The decentralization of blockchain means that instead of being stored in a single central server, copies of the blockchain ledger are held on multiple computers across the globe. This distribution of data not only makes tampering with recorded transactions challenging but practically impossible without being noticed by other participants in the network. Moreover, the encryption used in blockchain adds another layer of security. Each transaction is securely linked to the one before and after it, and to alter any piece of information, one would need to alter all subsequent entries, which is computationally impractical.

As the cryptocurrency landscape continues to evolve, so too do the security challenges associated with it. One emerging threat is the potential impact of quantum computing. Quantum computers, which are still in the early stages of development, theoretically can process tasks at speeds unimaginable to current standards, potentially enabling them to break the cryptographic algorithms that currently protect blockchain transactions. This possibility suggests a future where blockchain technology may need to adapt to resist quantum attacks by upgrading to quantum-resistant cryptographic algorithms.

Another future challenge lies in the increasing sophistication of cyber-attacks. As technologies evolve, so do the tactics of cybercriminals, who continually develop new methods to exploit system vulnerabilities. The cryptocurrency community must stay vigilant, continuously updating and strengthening security measures. This includes regular software updates, audits, and the adoption of emerging technologies that enhance security.

Navigating the complexities of cybersecurity in the cryptocurrency world is no small feat. Yet, by understanding the common threats and adopting vigorous security measures, you can protect your digital assets and personal information effectively. As you continue to explore the vast possibilities that cryptocurrencies offer, remember that your security practices can significantly impact your success and safety in this digital frontier.

The Future of National and Digital Currencies

As we navigate through the evolving landscape of finance, one of the most significant developments we're witnessing is the adoption of digital currencies by central banks around the world. These central bank digital currencies (CBDCs) are state-controlled alternatives to traditional paper money and even decentralized cryptocurrencies like Bitcoin. Unlike their decentralized counterparts, CBDCs are not a scheme to escape governmental oversight; instead, they are an embodiment of it, offering nations a new tool to maintain financial sovereignty and improve monetary policies.

The development of CBDCs is gaining momentum, with countries like China testing the Digital Yuan and the European Central Bank exploring a Digital Euro. These digital currencies aim to offer the benefits of cryptocurrencies—speed, security, and digital transferability—while maintaining the regulated, stable value of traditional currencies. The potential impacts on the global financial system are profound. CBDCs could streamline cross-border transactions, reduce transaction costs, and provide an alternative to the U.S. dollar for global trade, which could alter international economic dynamics significantly.

Switching gears, let's consider the distinctions between decentralized cryptocurrencies and state-controlled digital currencies. The former operates on a distributed ledger technology without centralized control, which fundamentally challenges the traditional, centralized system of financial governance. This decentralization offers advantages such as reduced transaction fees and greater user autonomy but also comes with challenges like price volatility and regulatory issues. On the other hand, digital currencies controlled by states offer stability and are backed by governmental monetary policies, yet they raise concerns about privacy and the potential for governmental overreach in financial transactions.

The integration of both types of digital currencies into the traditional banking system is an unfolding story. We're beginning to see a hybrid approach where banks are exploring blockchain technology to enhance efficiencies and reduce costs. This integration is likely to expand further as regulatory frameworks around cryptocurrencies mature and technological solutions are developed to bridge the gap between different types of currencies. The future could see banks maintaining balances in both fiat and digital currencies, seamlessly operating in a dual-currency environment to meet the diverse needs of their customers.

Speculating on what the future holds, it's expected that technological advancements will continue to drive the evolution of both national and digital currencies. User adoption rates will play a crucial role in shaping this landscape. As more people become comfortable using digital currencies and as the technology becomes more integrated into everyday financial activities, we can expect these currencies to become a staple in financial portfolios. Moreover, global economic conditions—such as inflation rates, economic growth, and geopolitical tensions—will influence the pace and nature of this adoption.

In navigating this future, we are not just passive observers but active participants. The choices we make, whether as consumers, investors, or policymakers, will shape the trajectory of these technologies and their impact on our global financial system. As we wrap up this exploration of the future of national and digital currencies, we're reminded of the broader implications of our topic. We're not merely discussing currency evolution; we're looking at a potential redefinition of economic sovereignty and personal financial agency in the digital age.

Moving forward into the next chapter, we will delve deeper into the technologies that underpin these developments. Understanding these will not only enhance our grasp of the current landscape but also empower us to make informed decisions as we navigate the future of digital finance.

Chapter 9

Mastering Crypto Taxation and Legal Issues

Imagine you've just found a treasure chest, but instead of gold coins, it's filled with various cryptocurrencies. You're thrilled at first, but then reality sets in—how do you manage this newfound wealth responsibly, especially when it comes to taxes? Navigating the labyrinth of cryptocurrency taxation isn't as daunting as it might seem, and understanding it can save you from unnecessary headaches and maximize your investments. Let's break down the essentials of crypto taxes and regulations in the U.S., ensuring you stay compliant and informed.

Understanding Crypto Taxes and Regulations in the US

Cryptocurrencies, despite their digital nature, aren't free from the grasp of taxation. The IRS treats cryptocurrencies as property in the United States, not currency. This classification has significant implications for your tax liabilities. Every time you sell, trade, or use cryptocurrencies to purchase goods, you're potentially creating a taxable event. The IRS requires you to report these events, and failure to do so could lead to penalties or audits.

Taxable Events

Let's dive deeper into what constitutes a taxable event in the realm of cryptocurrency. The most common events include:

- Trading Crypto: Swapping one cryptocurrency for another is a taxable event, where you realize capital gains or losses based on the value differences between the traded assets.

- Spending Crypto: Using cryptocurrencies to purchase goods or services also triggers a capital gains tax, calculated from the difference between the price you acquired the asset and its value at the time of the transaction.

- Mining Crypto: If you're mining cryptocurrencies, the fair market value of the coins at the time of delivery will be considered as taxable income.

- Earning Crypto: Earning cryptocurrencies through services or as payment for goods also counts as taxable income, based on the value of the crypto at the time it was received.

Understanding these events is crucial for managing your tax obligations effectively. Each event has its nuances, and how you report them can significantly affect your tax outcomes.

State vs. Federal Regulations

While federal tax requirements are consistent across the U.S., state regulations can vary dramatically. Some states treat cryptocurrency transactions more favorably than others. For instance, certain states have exempted cryptocurrencies from state securities laws, making them more attractive to crypto investors and businesses. Conversely, others have stricter regulations that might complicate tax reporting or operational compliance. It's essential to be aware of the regulations specific to your state, ensuring you adhere to both federal and state tax laws.

Recent IRS Updates and Guidance

Keeping up-to-date with IRS guidelines is critical as the landscape of cryptocurrency taxation evolves. The IRS has been refining its policies to address the complexities and nuances of crypto transactions. Recent updates have clarified the reporting requirements for specific scenarios, such as hard forks, airdrops, and the tax treatment of staking rewards. These updates aim to provide clearer guidance for taxpayers, ensuring they understand their obligations and can report their transactions accurately.

For instance, the IRS's recent guidance on hard forks and airdrops clarifies that if new cryptocurrencies are created and you have control over them, their fair market value must be reported as ordinary income. This guidance is crucial for anyone involved in cryptocurrency activities, as it impacts how you assess and report your income.

Navigating the maze of cryptocurrency taxation might seem overwhelming at first, but with a proper understanding of the rules and regulations, you can manage your crypto assets wisely. Staying informed and compliant not only helps you avoid legal pitfalls but also empowers you to make the most of your investments in this dynamic digital landscape. Remember, knowledge is not just power in the world of cryptocurrency—it's profit.

How to Report Crypto on Your Taxes

When it comes to dealing with cryptocurrencies, whether you're a casual investor or an expert trader, one of the most vital aspects to keep on top of is how to report your crypto transactions on your taxes. The first step in this process is meticulous documentation.

Every transaction you make, from selling Bitcoin to using Ethereum to buy a coffee, needs to be recorded. You should note the date of each transaction, the amounts involved, the market value of the crypto at the time of the transaction, and any fees you paid. This might sound tedious, but it's crucial for accurate tax reporting. Each piece of data plays a critical role in determining your tax obligations and can help you minimize your tax liability legally.

Let's dive deeper into why each piece of information is important. The date of the transaction establishes when the tax liability is incurred, which is essential for calculating holding periods that determine whether gains are taxed as short-term or long-term. This can significantly affect the tax rate applied, as the amount and market value are necessary in calculating your gain or loss from each transaction. For instance, if you bought Bitcoin at $35,000 and sold it at $40,000, your gain would be $5,000, which is subject to capital gains tax. Transaction fees, while often overlooked, can also affect the cost basis of your crypto, potentially reducing the taxable gain when you sell it.

Moving onto the tax forms, if you've engaged in crypto transactions throughout the year, you'll likely need to familiarize yourself with IRS Form 8949 and Schedule D. Form 8949 is where you list all transactions involving capital assets, including cryptocurrencies. Here, you'll detail each transaction and report the date acquired, date sold, proceeds, cost basis, and gain or loss. Schedule D is used to summarize your total losses or capital gains reported on Form 8949. If you've just dabbled in crypto and only have a few transactions, this might seem straightforward. However, if you're a frequent trader or have numerous transactions, this can quickly become complex.

This complexity is why many turn to tax software and tools designed to handle cryptocurrency transactions. These tools can automatically import your transactions from various exchanges via API access or through transaction history files you upload. They then calculate your gains and losses, taking into account the dates and values of each transaction. Some popular options include CoinTracker, CryptoTrader, Tax, and ZenLedger, which offer a range of features, from simple gain and loss calculations to complete tax preparation services. However, they're not without limitations. Most require a subscription fee, and their accuracy depends heavily on the completeness of the transaction data they can access. If you've used multiple exchanges or have private transactions, ensuring the software has a complete record can be challenging.

Given the complexities and the potential for significant financial implications, many crypto investors choose to consult with a tax professional. This is especially advisable if you have a large volume of transactions, participate in activities like staking or mining, or if you receive airdrops or rewards. Tax professionals specializing in cryptocurrency can provide tailored advice that considers the latest tax laws and your specific situation. They can help ensure that you're taking advantage of all available tax strategies, such as identifying which cryptocurrencies to sell to optimize your tax liability based on holding periods and cost basis. They can also assist in situations where you might need to amend past returns due to incorrectly reported crypto transactions—a not uncommon scenario given the evolving nature of crypto tax guidance.

In essence, the process of documenting and reporting your cryptocurrency transactions for tax purposes, while potentially daunting, is a crucial aspect of managing your investments.

Thorough record-keeping, understanding which tax forms to use, utilizing robust tax software, and, when necessary, enlisting the help of a professional are all steps that will help you navigate the complexities of crypto taxation. With these practices in place, you can focus more on your investment strategies and less on administrative burdens, ensuring that you remain compliant while optimizing your financial outcomes.

Legal Challenges in Cryptocurrency Ownership and Transfer

When you hold cryptocurrencies, it's not just about keeping track of your digital assets; it's also about understanding the complex legal landscape that governs their ownership and transfer. One of the foundational aspects of owning cryptocurrency is grasping the concept of ownership rights and proof. Unlike traditional assets, where proof of ownership might involve a physical deed or a certificate, cryptocurrencies are entirely digital, and ownership is defined by who holds the private keys. These keys enable you to access and control your cryptocurrency. Therefore, maintaining the security of your private keys is paramount. Think of your private keys like the combination to a safe—except this safe holds your digital wealth. If you lose access to your private keys, you effectively lose ownership of your cryptocurrency with no way to retrieve it because there's no central authority or system to appeal to for recovery.

Moreover, the security of your digital assets doesn't just hinge on keeping your private keys safe from loss—it also involves safeguarding them from unauthorized access. This is where the legal aspect comes into play. If someone else gains access to them without your permission, the decentralized and anonymous nature of blockchain can make it nearly impossible to recover your assets.

This is why employing robust security measures, such as using hardware wallets to store your private keys offline, is crucial.

Additionally, understanding and using the technology correctly is critical to ensure that you do not inadvertently expose your private keys while transacting online.

Now, let's consider the complexities of smart contracts. These self-executing contracts have the terms written into code, then stored and replicated on the blockchain, and supervised by the computer network running the blockchain. This technology allows parties to transact securely and transparently without an intermediary. However, the enforceability of smart contracts under current law presents potential challenges, especially in dispute resolutions and contractual obligations. For instance, what happens if there's a bug in the code that executes a different transaction than agreed upon? Or if one party finds a way to exploit a loophole in the contract's code to their advantage? The decentralized nature of blockchain means there's no central authority to arbitrate such disputes, which could complicate legal proceedings.

Furthermore, as smart contracts are relatively new and the laws surrounding them are still developing, not all jurisdictions may recognize them as legally binding agreements.

This can lead to challenges in enforcing the terms of a smart contract in a court of law, should the need arise. As the use of smart contracts becomes more widespread, we can expect more legal frameworks to adapt and provide clearer guidelines on their usage. However, until then, parties using smart contracts should be cautious and consider seeking legal advice to understand the risks and how they might be mitigated.

Moving on to estate planning and inheritance, cryptocurrencies present unique challenges. Given their digital nature and the fact that they are not held in traditional bank accounts, they can be easily overlooked or forgotten after the owner's death. To prevent this, it's crucial to include your digital assets in your estate planning. This involves ensuring that detailed instructions about accessing your cryptocurrencies are available to your heirs without compromising the security of your private keys. Consider using a service that allows you to securely store your digital asset information in a way that it can only be accessed by your beneficiaries upon your death.

Finally, cross-border legal issues are another significant area of concern for cryptocurrency owners. Different countries have varied regulations regarding cryptocurrencies, which can affect everything from your ability to conduct transactions to your obligations for reporting for tax purposes. For instance, some countries may have strict capital controls that prohibit or limit the transfer of cryptocurrencies across borders or may apply different tax treatments to gains made from cryptocurrency transactions. Additionally, the global nature of cryptocurrencies and the potential for them to be used in international transactions can complicate compliance with international anti-money laundering (AML) and counter-terrorism financing (CTF) laws.

Navigating these complex legal challenges requires staying informed about the latest regulations in your area and any others you interact with. It also involves taking proactive steps to secure your assets and plan for the future. As the legal landscape around cryptocurrencies continues to evolve, staying adaptable and informed will be the key to successfully managing your digital assets.

International Crypto Laws: What Investors Should Know

Navigating the international landscape of cryptocurrency laws can often feel like trying to find your way through a labyrinth. Each country has its own set of rules and regulations, which can significantly affect your decisions and strategies as an investor. For instance, while some countries embrace cryptocurrencies with open arms and minimal regulation, others impose strict controls or outright bans. Understanding these differences is crucial for anyone involved in the international crypto market.

In the European Union, the regulatory environment is particularly complex due to the convergence of member states' laws with EU-wide regulations. A significant aspect of EU regulations that affect cryptocurrencies is the General Data Protection Regulation (GDPR), which imposes strict rules on the handling of personal data. Given that blockchains are inherently transparent and immutable, reconciling GDPR requirements with blockchain technology presents a unique challenge. For instance, the GDPR's "right to be forgotten," which allows individuals to request the deletion of personal data, seems at odds with the blockchain's permanent record-keeping. This discord has prompted ongoing discussions and developments within the EU to find a balanced approach that respects both privacy rights and the technological framework of cryptocurrencies.

Moreover, compliance with Anti-Money Laundering (AML) and Counter-Terrorism Financing (CTF) laws is a universal requirement across jurisdictions. These laws are designed to prevent illicit activities such as money laundering and terrorist financing, and they apply to cryptocurrency transactions just as they do to traditional financial transactions. Compliance involves performing due diligence on customers (often referred to as Know Your Customer or KYC procedures) by monitoring transactions for suspicious activities and reporting to regulatory bodies as necessary. The penalties for non-compliance can be severe, ranging from hefty fines to operational shutdowns, making it imperative for crypto businesses and investors to adhere strictly to these regulations.

Navigating tax obligations in the international arena can be particularly tricky. Each country has its own tax rules regarding cryptocurrencies, and these can vary widely. For example, some countries treat gains from cryptocurrencies as capital gains, while others might treat them as income, each with different tax implications. Furthermore, if you are a resident of one country but transact on an exchange based in another, you may be subject to tax obligations in both jurisdictions. Managing these obligations requires a careful understanding of the tax laws applicable to each transaction and jurisdiction. Strategies to manage potential tax liabilities include using accounting methods that optimize tax outcomes, such as choosing specific identification of coins sold to control which gains are realized.

Cryptocurrencies continue to gain popularity, so we can expect further developments in international regulations. Keeping abreast of changes is essential for anyone engaged in the global cryptocurrency market. Staying informed can help you navigate the complexities of international crypto laws, ensuring compliance and optimizing your investment strategy.

Reflecting on what we've covered in this chapter, it's clear that the landscape of crypto taxation and legal issues is both complex and dynamic. From understanding the intricacies of U.S. tax requirements to navigating the global regulatory environment, the need for diligent management and a proactive approach is evident. As we move forward, the intersection of technology, law, and finance will likely continue to evolve, presenting both challenges and opportunities. By staying informed and adaptable, you can navigate these waters successfully, ensuring compliance while maximizing your investment potential.

As we close this chapter on the legal and tax intricacies of cryptocurrencies, we turn our attention to the future. The next chapter will explore emerging trends and technologies in the crypto space. We'll look at what's on the horizon for digital currencies and blockchain technology, preparing you to navigate and leverage these advancements effectively.

Chapter 10

Staying Ahead in the Crypto World

Imagine the crypto world as a vast, ever-changing landscape, where today's lush valley might be tomorrow's mountain peak—or vice versa. Staying ahead in this dynamic environment isn't just about keeping up; it's about actively engaging with the continuous flow of information and learning. In this chapter, we'll explore how you can maintain your edge by developing a robust learning routine, diversifying your educational resources, making wise use of social media, and connecting with the community through conferences and meetups.

Keeping Up with Crypto: Best Practices for Continuous Learning

Establishing a Learning Routine

Your journey through the crypto world can be thrilling, but without a map and a compass, it's easy to lose your way. Establishing a learning routine is like setting up a navigation system that keeps you on the right path. This routine should include daily or weekly habits such as reading leading crypto news websites to ensure you're up to date with market trends and technological advancements. Websites like CoinDesk, Cointelegraph, and CryptoSlate offer timely and detailed articles that cover everything from market analysis to regulatory news.

Additionally, tuning into updates from influential crypto analysts and thought leaders can provide deeper insights and diverse perspectives that help refine your understanding and strategies. Podcasts and YouTube channels, such as "Unchained" by Laura Shin or "The Pomp Podcast" by Anthony Pompliano, feature interviews with industry experts and discussions on complex topics made accessible. Regularly monitoring these sources will not only keep you informed but also enhance your ability to anticipate market movements and make informed decisions.

Engaging with Educational Content

While staying updated on the news is crucial, deepening your knowledge through structured learning is equally important. The crypto and blockchain space is rich with educational content that ranges from books and online courses to webinars and workshops. For example, enrolling in courses offered by platforms like Coursera, Udemy, or the CryptoCurrency Certification Consortium (C4) can provide you with a structured and comprehensive understanding of various aspects of blockchain technology and cryptocurrency investing.

Diversifying your learning resources ensures that you're not only getting a wide range of information but also accessing multiple teaching styles that can help reinforce your learning. For instance, attending webinars and interactive workshops not only provides visual and auditory learning but also allows you to ask questions and engage in discussions, thereby enhancing your understanding and retention of information.

Using Social Media Wisely

Social media platforms, such as Reddit, Twitter, and LinkedIn, are treasure troves of information and community engagement—if used wisely. They offer real-time updates, trending discussions, and direct interactions with leaders and enthusiasts in the crypto space. To make the most out of social media, follow reputable accounts of crypto analysts, influencers, and news outlets. Engage in communities like r/CryptoCurrency or LinkedIn groups dedicated to blockchain technology to exchange ideas and get diverse opinions.

However, the key is to remain critical of the information you consume. The open nature of social media allows for a mix of insightful content and misinformation. Always cross-reference news and tips with credible sources and avoid making investment decisions based exclusively on social media trends. Being selective and thoughtful about your sources on these platforms can turn them into valuable tools for learning and networking.

Attending Crypto Conferences and Meetups

Nothing beats the immersive experience of attending crypto conferences and meetups. These events are not just about listening to talks but also about engaging with a community of like-minded individuals who are equally passionate about the future of cryptocurrencies. Conferences like Consensus or the North American Bitcoin Conference bring together industry leaders, innovators, and investors and provide a wealth of knowledge and networking opportunities.

Meetups in your local area can be found on platforms like Meetup. com, offering more frequent and accessible opportunities to connect with local crypto enthusiasts. These gatherings can be invaluable for sharing experiences, discussing strategies, and even forming partnerships. The benefits of attending these events extend beyond just gaining knowledge; they also embed you within a community that can support and inspire you as you navigate the complex world of cryptocurrency.

By integrating these practices into your routine, you are not only staying informed but also actively participating in the crypto community. This proactive approach to learning and engagement will provide you with the knowledge and connections to thrive in the ever-evolving cryptocurrency landscape.

Participating in Crypto Communities and Forums

Engaging with online communities and forums dedicated to cryptocurrency can transform your understanding and approach to investing. These platforms are more than just spaces for discussion— they are vibrant ecosystems where novices and experts alike converge to share insights, strategies, and firsthand experiences. Selecting the right communities is crucial; you want to be part of groups that are not only active but also informative. Cryptocurrency forums, Discord servers, and specialized Telegram groups are excellent starting points. Look for communities that foster a culture of helpfulness and are known for their knowledgeable members. The quality of discourse can significantly vary, so it's beneficial to spend some time lurking in these groups to gauge the depth and relevance of the discussions before fully engaging.

Once you've found communities that resonate with your needs, understanding and adhering to netiquette—internet etiquette—is vital. Every community has its set of rules, often explicitly stated, but there's also an unwritten code of conduct based on respect and constructive communication. For instance, it's good practice to search the forum before posting questions to avoid duplicates, which clutter the platform and can frustrate regular users. Engage respectfully, appreciating that behind every username is a person who might be more or less knowledgeable than you are. Constructive disagreement over different investment strategies or interpretations of market behavior is beneficial; it exposes you to new perspectives and deepens your understanding. However, these discussions should always be conducted respectfully and without personal attacks.

Active participation in these communities is not just about taking in information but also contributing to discussions. Start by responding to others' posts with thoughtful comments or insightful questions. Once you feel more confident, initiate discussions or share articles that you find compelling and think might help others. This proactive engagement is beneficial for several reasons. Firstly, it enables you to clarify your own thoughts and refine your strategies by articulating them to others. Secondly, it builds your reputation in the community, opening up more opportunities for deeper engagement and networking. Over time, you might find yourself in conversations with thought leaders or seasoned investors whose advice could be instrumental in shaping your investment approaches.

Learning from community experiences is perhaps one of the most valuable aspects of participating in crypto forums and groups. Members often share their successes and, more importantly, their mistakes. These narratives are goldmines of practical advice, offering unfiltered insights into the realities of cryptocurrency investment and security practices. For example, a common discussion might revolve around the pitfalls of failing to secure one's digital wallet or falling prey to phishing scams. These stories provide real-life lessons on what to do and what not to do, serving as both warnings and educational tools. By understanding and internalizing these experiences, you can avoid common errors and make informed decisions in your crypto ventures.

Moreover, some of the most enlightening moments in these forums come from collaborative problem-solving. When members encounter complex challenges or unique scenarios, the collective expertise of the community can come together to provide solutions and ideas that no individual might have considered. This collaborative environment not only helps solve individual issues but also contributes to the collective knowledge base, enhancing the overall sophistication and savviness of the community.

In essence, engaging with the right crypto communities and forums can significantly enhance your learning curve and improve your effectiveness as a crypto investor or enthusiast. By choosing active and informative platforms, respecting community etiquette, actively contributing to discussions, and learning from collective experiences, you can gain a wealth of knowledge and insights that are rarely found in textbooks or traditional courses. These interactions provide a dynamic learning environment that keeps pace with the swiftly evolving world of cryptocurrency, preparing you to navigate its complexities with greater confidence and competence.

Future Trends: What Next for Cryptocurrencies?

As we look toward the horizon of the cryptocurrency sector, it's clear that the landscape is poised for significant evolution, driven by advancements in technology and shifts in regulatory and environmental paradigms. One of the most compelling technological frontiers is quantum computing. Unlike traditional computing, which uses bits as the smallest unit of data, quantum computing uses qubits. This allows them to perform complex calculations at speeds unattainable by current standards, potentially decrypting algorithms that keep cryptocurrencies like Bitcoin secure. While this poses a risk, it also catalyzes the crypto community to innovate on quantum-resistant blockchain technologies, ensuring that your digital assets remain safe against even the most cutting-edge adversarial technologies.

In parallel, Artificial Intelligence (AI) integration is set to redefine how blockchain operates. AI can optimize mining processes, enhance security protocols, and even make autonomous trading decisions. By analyzing vast amounts of data and recognizing patterns faster than any human, AI systems could potentially predict market trends and provide investors with incredibly accurate insights. This integration could lead to smarter, more efficient blockchain networks that are both more secure and more profitable for those who understand how to leverage these AI capabilities.

Furthermore, scalability remains a critical challenge for blockchain technology. The Lightning Network for Bitcoin is a second-layer solution and offers promising remedies. These protocols operate on top of a blockchain to enable faster transactions and better scalability by handling transactions off the main chain while still maintaining security and decentralization. This could mean that in the future, you could use cryptocurrencies for everyday purchases, such as coffee or groceries, without experiencing delays and high transaction fees, making digital currencies more practical for everyday use by mainstream consumers.

Predicting market movements has always been part of the crypto investor's toolkit, but with the advent of algorithmic trading and predictive analytics, this process is becoming more sophisticated. Algorithmic trading uses mathematical models to make transaction decisions, executing orders at speeds and frequencies that are challenging for human traders. When combined with predictive analytics, which uses real-time and historical data to predict future market trends, investors can make more informed decisions. These tools are becoming increasingly accessible to the average investor, leveling the playing field between institutional investors and individual traders.

On the regulatory front, the landscape is continually evolving. As cryptocurrencies gain popularity, governments around the world are beginning to recognize the need for regulation to mitigate risks such as fraud, money laundering, and market manipulation. However, there's a delicate balance to strike. Over-regulation could stifle innovation and the growth of cryptocurrencies, while under-regulation could lead to investor harm and financial instability. Future regulatory frameworks will likely focus on enhancing transparency, improving security standards, and protecting investors, all while ensuring that the innovative spirit of the crypto world remains unhindered.

Lastly, the sustainability of cryptocurrency operations is becoming a priority. The traditional model of crypto mining is energy-intensive, contributing to carbon emissions and environmental degradation. However, the industry is shifting towards more sustainable practices, including the use of renewable energy sources such as solar, wind, and hydroelectric power. Innovations like green blockchain technologies and energy-efficient consensus algorithms like Proof of Stake (PoS) are gaining traction. These developments are not just good for the planet; they also offer a more sustainable path forward for the growth of cryptocurrencies, ensuring that the digital asset space can continue to expand without contributing disproportionately to environmental issues.

These emerging trends and technologies herald a transformative phase in the cryptocurrency sector, promising to make digital currencies more secure, efficient, and integrated into everyday financial activities. As these advancements unfold, staying informed and adaptable will be vital in successfully navigating the future landscape of cryptocurrencies.

Investing in Crypto Startups: Risks and Rewards

Investing in crypto startups is akin to planting seeds in a garden that's still being mapped out; it's filled with potential but requires patience, nurturing, and a deep understanding of the landscape to thrive. When you're looking to invest in these burgeoning companies, the first step is evaluating their viability. This isn't just about checking their current market performance or funding rounds; it involves a deeper analysis of their business models, the specific needs they aim to meet within the market, their technological innovations, and the expertise of their team.

Start by examining the business model of the crypto startup. What problem is it solving, and how does it intend to solve it? Is there an obvious demand for this solution in the crypto market? These questions help you gauge the practicality and potential longevity of the startup. For instance, a crypto venture that aims to enhance blockchain scalability is addressing a clear, existing issue that could improve how systems operate, indicating a strong market need. Next, look at the technology itself—is it innovative, and more importantly, is it feasible? Cutting-edge technology that's not practical or is too ahead of its time might not achieve commercial success. Lastly, a competent and experienced team is crucial. The presence of skilled professionals who have navigated similar arenas or have a strong track record in tech and business leadership is often a promising sign that they can steer the startup toward success.

The avenues for investing in crypto startups are diverse, each carrying its unique flavor of risk and potential reward. The sale of tokens, also known as Initial Coin Offerings (ICOs), is widespread. This allows startups to raise capital and issue their own digital currency, which can be used on their platform or traded on crypto exchanges. While ICOs can offer high returns, they are also risky, especially if the tokens don't gain market traction or the project fails to develop as promised. Equity investments are another pathway, where you buy a share of the company itself, giving you a potentially stable investment tied to the company's overall success and a vote in major decisions. Crowdfunding platforms represent a more accessible option, allowing you to invest smaller amounts in various startups, spreading your risks while still supporting innovative projects.

When diving into startup investments, managing risk is paramount. Diversification is critical—spread your investments across various sectors within the crypto world, such as mining, blockchain development, or financial services, to mitigate risks associated with any single area. Setting clear investment goals and understanding your own risk tolerance can guide your investment choices, helping you decide how much to invest and when to exit. Legal implications are also critical; ensure you understand the regulatory environment as it can impact startup operations and your rights as an investor.

Exploring case studies of both successful and failed crypto startups can provide invaluable lessons. Take the example of a successful startup like Binance, which grew from an ICO to a significant global digital currency exchange. Key factors in its success included addressing a clear market need for more secure and efficient crypto trading platforms, a strong leadership team, and robust technology. On the flip side, consider the cautionary tale of BitConnect, a platform that promised high returns on investment through its trading bot but was ultimately shut down after being accused of creating a Ponzi scheme. This case highlights the importance of due diligence and the risks of high-yield investment promises in the crypto space.

By understanding these dynamics, you can better navigate the exciting yet complex terrain of crypto startup investments, making informed decisions that align with your financial goals and risk tolerance. Engaging with this emerging market offers the dual thrill of potential financial reward and the opportunity to be part of innovative projects that could shape the future of technology. As you consider your next steps, remember that, like any investment, clarity, strategy, and continuous learning are your best tools for success.

Leveraging Augmented Reality for Cryptocurrency Learning

Augmented Reality (AR) is a technology that overlays digital information onto the real world, enhancing your perception of reality through devices like smartphones or AR glasses. This fusion of digital and real-world elements creates engaging and interactive experiences that can transform educational methods, especially in complex fields like cryptocurrency. By integrating AR into crypto education, learners can visualize and interact with abstract concepts such as blockchain operations, cryptocurrency mining, and trading processes in a more tangible way, making these topics more accessible and easier to understand.

The application of AR in crypto education is still in its emerging stage, but it shows promising potential. For instance, imagine an AR application that visually represents the blockchain process right on your table. You could watch a virtual block being added to the chain every time a transaction is verified, with each block displaying real-time data. This kind of immersive experience could significantly enhance your understanding of how blockchains operate. Another application could be in the realm of crypto trading, where AR tools project market data into your physical space, allowing you to interact with live charts or manipulate data points in a three-dimensional space. Such tools not only make learning about cryptocurrencies more interactive but also more engaging, helping to retain complex information more effectively.

For educators and developers looking to create AR learning modules tailored to cryptocurrency education, the focus should be on interactivity and user engagement. The development process involves several stages, starting with the identification of key learning objectives. For example, if the goal is to explain how smart contracts work, the AR experience might involve a step-by-step simulation of creating and executing a smart contract. Developers must then design intuitive user interfaces that allow learners to interact with the information seamlessly. This might include touch gestures for mobile AR applications or voice commands for more immersive AR headsets. Moreover, integrating gamification elements such as scores, challenges, or unlockable content can further enhance engagement and motivation.

The future of AR in financial education, particularly in teaching about cryptocurrencies, looks incredibly promising. As AR technology continues to advance, its integration into educational tools is likely to become more sophisticated, offering more immersive and interactive learning experiences. This could revolutionize how complex financial concepts are taught, making them more understandable and accessible to a broader audience. Moreover, as cryptocurrencies and blockchain technology play a more prominent role in the global financial system, the demand for innovative educational approaches that can cater to all levels of expertise and backgrounds is expected to grow. AR could play a crucial role in meeting this educational demand, providing a bridge between complex technical knowledge and everyday understanding.

Incorporating AR into cryptocurrency education not only aids in comprehension but also prepares you for a future where technology blends more seamlessly with finance. As you continue to explore the multifaceted world of cryptocurrencies, the use of augmented reality in learning can be a powerful tool for demystifying complex concepts and enhancing your overall understanding. This engaging approach to learning not only makes education more effective but also more enjoyable, potentially attracting more individuals to the field of cryptocurrencies and fostering a more informed and savvy community of users and investors.

In wrapping up this exploration of augmented reality in cryptocurrency education, we've seen how AR can transform traditional learning methods by making complex concepts more tangible and engaging. This chapter has highlighted the potential of AR to not only enhance understanding but also to make learning about cryptocurrencies accessible to a broader audience. As we move forward, the intersection of AR technology with crypto education promises to be an exciting area of growth, offering new ways to learn, interact, and engage with the digital economy. As we continue to navigate the evolving landscape of cryptocurrencies, embracing innovative technologies like AR will be the key to staying informed and ahead in the game.

Moving into the next chapter, we'll delve into the practical aspects of applying the knowledge you've gained about cryptocurrencies, focusing on strategies for effective investment and portfolio management. This next step will equip you with the tools to not only understand but also actively participate in the cryptocurrency market, applying your learning to make informed investment decisions.

Conclusion

What a journey we've been on together! From the early pages, where we unpacked the basics of cryptocurrency and blockchain technology, to diving deep into advanced investment strategies and market analysis techniques, our exploration has been both broad and intensive. We started with fundamental concepts, understanding how digital currencies operate on decentralized platforms, and gradually advanced to mastering the tools and tactics that seasoned investors use to navigate the complex crypto markets.

Throughout this book, my aim has been to empower you with knowledge—knowledge that not only enhances your understanding but also equips you with the necessary tools to navigate the cryptocurrency space with confidence. By now, you should feel more prepared to make informed investment decisions and tackle the challenges that come with this dynamic market.

However, as we've discussed, the world of cryptocurrency never stands still. The rapid pace of innovation and the continuous evolution of technology mean that learning is an ongoing process. Staying updated with the latest developments and adapting to new technologies and regulations is crucial. It's a world that rewards the curious and the diligent—those who are willing to keep learning and evolving alongside the market itself.

The potential of cryptocurrencies extends far beyond their use as investment vehicles.

Throughout our chapters, we've seen how these digital assets are making significant impacts across various sectors, including finance and healthcare, and even by addressing societal challenges. This transformative power underscores the importance of understanding and engaging with cryptocurrencies not just for personal gain but also for their broader implications.

Yet, with great potential comes great responsibility. The volatility, the ever-changing regulatory landscapes, cybersecurity threats, and environmental concerns are real challenges that require us to approach cryptocurrency investment with care and responsibility. It's crucial to practice due diligence, employ robust risk management strategies, and make ethical investment choices that consider the long-term impacts on our community and planet.

I encourage you not just to invest but to become an active participant in cryptocurrency communities. Share your knowledge, learn from others, and contribute to a collective understanding and responsible growth of this exciting field. Engage in forums, attend meetups, and stay connected with the pulse of the crypto world.

As we look to the future, let your curiosity about emerging trends such as Decentralized Finance (DeFi), Non-Fungible Tokens (NFTs), and beyond guide you to new opportunities and innovations. The horizon is continually expanding, and the possibilities are as limitless as your willingness to explore them.

I sincerely hope this book has provided you with a solid foundation and that it serves as a springboard for your continued success in cryptocurrency investing.

Thank you for trusting me to be your guide on this incredible adventure. Here's to taking bold steps, making informed decisions, and building wealth in the ever-evolving world of cryptocurrencies. Stay curious, stay cautious, and above all, stay engaged. Happy investing!

References

- *Bitcoin, Blockchain and the History of Money* https://www.imf.org/en/Publications/fandd/issues/2018/06/bitcoin-blockchain-history-of-money-james

- *What is Blockchain Technology? How Does Blockchain Work ...* https://www.simplilearn.com/tutorials/blockchain-tutorial/blockchain-technology#:~:text=Blockchain%20is%20a%20method%20of,computers%20participating%20in%20the%20blockchain.

- *Cryptocurrency vs. Traditional Banking: Understanding the ...* https://www.globaltrademag.com/cryptocurrency-vs-traditional-banking-understanding-the-differences-and-benefits/

- *Cryptocurrency Regulations Around the World* https://www.investopedia.com/cryptocurrency-regulations-around-the-world-5202122

- *What Is a Crypto Wallet and How to Choose the Right One?* https://academy.binance.com/en/articles/crypto-wallet-types-explained

- *undefined* undefined

- *What To Know About Cryptocurrency and Scams* https://consumer.ftc.gov/articles/what-know-about-cryptocurrency-and-scams

- *7 Best Cryptocurrency Investing Strategies* https://money.usnews.com/investing/articles/best-cryptocurrency-investing-strategies

- *The 8 best indicators for crypto trading in 2024* https://www.okx.com/learn/best-crypto-indicators-trading

- *How To Read Crypto Candlestick Charts* https://www.ledger.com/academy/crypto-candlestick-charts-explained

- *undefined* undefined

- *How to Create a Well-Balanced Crypto Portfolio* https://www.fool.com/investing/stock-market/market-sectors/financials/cryptocurrency-stocks/crypto-portfolio/

- *Crypto Users Lost $2B to Hacks, Scams and Exploits in ...* https://www.coindesk.com/tech/2023/12/27/crypto-users-lost-2b-to-hacks-scams-and-exploits-in-2023-defi-says/

- *Crypto Regulations in the US—A Complete Guide (2023)* https://sumsub.com/blog/crypto-regulations-in-the-us-a-complete-guide-2023/

- *What To Know About Cryptocurrency and Scams* https://consumer.ftc.gov/articles/what-know-about-cryptocurrency-and-scams

- *5 Ways to Manage Risk When Trading Cryptocurrency* https://www.coindesk.com/learn/how-to-manage-risk-when-trading-cryptocurrency/

- *undefined* undefined

- *What Is DeFi? Understanding Decentralized Finance* https://www.forbes.com/advisor/investing/cryptocurrency/defi-decentralized-finance/

- *Crypto Staking Explained: How It Works, Types, & Risks* https://www.britannica.com/money/what-is-crypto-staking

- *How to Participate in ICOs and Token Sales - Cryptomus* https://cryptomus.com/blog/how-to-participate-in-icos-and-token-sales-a-comprehensive-guide

- *Crypto Technical Analysis: Techniques, Indicators, and ...* https://onetrading.com/blogs/crypto-technical-analysis-techniques-indicators-and-applications

- *Valuation of Cryptoassets: A Guide for Investment ...* https://rpc.cfainstitute.org/en/research/reports/2023/valuation-cryptoassets

- *Do investor sentiments drive cryptocurrency prices?* https://www.sciencedirect.com/science/article/abs/pii/S0165176521002573

- *The Impact of Global Economic Indicators on Crypto Prices* https://medium.com/@maulanaazizi/the-impact-of-global-economic-indicators-on-crypto-prices-an-in-depth-analysis-a4d26c48c0d6

- *Top 5 Real-World Use Cases of Blockchain in Healthcare Organizations* https://www.linkedin.com/pulse/top-5-real-world-use-cases-blockchain-healthcare-organizations

- *Best Smart Contract Use Cases Across Industries in 2024* https://pixelplex.io/blog/smart-contract-use-cases/

- *Crypto Remittances: How Cryptocurrency Is Transforming ...* https://blog.bake.io/crypto-remittances/

- *9 Nonprofits Harnessing Blockchain For Social Impact* https://thegivingblock.com/resources/nonprofits-using-blockchain-social-impact/

- *Debunking the narratives about cryptocurrency and financial inclusion* https://www.brookings.edu/articles/debunking-the-narratives-about-cryptocurrency-and-financial-inclusion/

- *The environmental impact of bitcoin mining explained* https://www.techtarget.com/sustainability/feature/The-environmental-impact-of-bitcoin-mining-explained

- *What to Know About Cryptocurrency and Cybersecurity Risks* https://www.cnb.com/personal-banking/insights/cryptocurrency-cybersecurity-risks.html

- *Central bank digital currency evolution in 2023 - Atlantic Council* https://www.atlanticcouncil.org/blogs/econographics/central-bank-digital-currency-evolution-in-2023-from-investigation-to-preparation/

- *Digital Assets | Internal Revenue Service* https://www.irs.gov/businesses/small-businesses-self-employed/digital-assets

- *GLOBAL CRYPTOASSET REGULATORY LANDSCAPE STUDY* https://www.jbs.cam.ac.uk/wp-content/uploads/2020/08/2019-04-ccaf-global-cryptoasset-regulatory-landscape-study.pdf

- *Best Crypto Tax Software Of May 2024* https://www.forbes.com/advisor/taxes/best-crypto-tax-software/

- *Estate Planning and Cryptocurrency* https://freemanlaw.com/estate-planning-and-cryptocurrency/

- *The 12 Best Crypto News Websites in 2024* https://coinledger.io/tools/best-crypto-news-sites

- *What To Know About Cryptocurrency and Scams* https://consumer.ftc.gov/articles/what-know-about-cryptocurrency-and-scams

- *List of the Top 30 Crypto & Blockchain Conferences in 2024* https://ninjapromo.io/best-crypto-conferences

- *Quantum Computing Could Threaten Blockchain, Crypto* https://news.bloomberglaw.com/us-law-week/quantum-computing-could-threaten-blockchain-crypto